·The· ISLAND KITCHEN

VOLUME TWO

more delicious recipes from

THE ISLE of MAN

Robinson's

A FAMILY BUSINESS SINCE 1886

THE ISLAND KITCHEN VOLUME TWO

Editors

Sara Donaldson attended the Robert Gordon University in Aberdeen. After working as a university librarian in her native North Yorkshire, she returned north and now enjoys life as an editor in the far north of Scotland. Her interests include art, history and cooking. When not working, she can usually be found in her local community theatre.

Emma Ames is currently enjoying the final year of her Publishing with English BA at Loughborough University. Her interests include theatre, historical and fantasy novels, food and creative writing. She looks forward to graduating and hopes to forge a career in the publishing industry.

Managing Editor: Miles Cowsill

Art Directors: Andrew Lowe, Miles Cowsill

Photography: Simon Park, Lily Publications, The Abbey Resturant and Dept of Environment, Food and Agriculture.

Acknowledgements: Nicola Green, Julie Blackburn, Andrew Lees, Audrey Fowler, Lucy Verdon, Laura Dalton and Angela Byrne.

Copyright 2019 Lily Publications Ltd. All right reserved
ISBN: 978-1-911177-55-5
Publisher: Lily Publications Ltd, PO Box 33, Ramsey, Isle of Man, IM99 4LP
Tel: +44 (0) 1624 898446 www.lilypublications.co.uk

Printed by Printer Trento, Italy

Contents

Introduction 9

Robinson's - A provenance in produce 10

Isle of Man food & drink 19

Restaurants

Douglas & the east

14 North 26

    14 North's starter **King scallop ceviche** 28

    14 North's main course **Pan-seared Gressingham duck breast** 31

    14 North's dessert **75% dark chocolate ganache** 35

Little Fish Cafe 38

    Little Fish Cafe's starter **Monkfish fritters** 40

    Little Fish Cafe's main course **Penang seafood curry** 43

    Little Fish Cafe's dessert **Flourless orange and almond cake** 49

The Courthouse 50

    Courthouse's starter **Seven Kingdom Douglas dry gin-cured salmon** 54

    Courthouse's main course **Manx pork fillet with Manx chorizo** 57

    Courthouse's dessert **Panna cotta fv elderflower wine, macerated strawberries and basil jelly** 58

Ocean 60

    Ocean's starter **Crab and courgette cannelloni** 62

    Ocean's main course **Roast salmon fillet with romesco sauce and crispy prawns** 64

    Ocean's dessert **Chocolate tart with raspberry sorbet and almond glass** 67

Tanroagan 70

    Tanroagan's starter **Crab toasties** 74

    Tanroagan's main course **Seabass involtini** 76

    Tanroagan's dessert **Limoncello cheesecake with icecream** 79

Alessandro's 80

    Alessandro's starter **Goat's cheese bon bons** 83

    Alessandro's main course **Thyme for fish** 84

    Alessandro's dessert **Summer tiramisu** 86

Enzo's 88

    Enzo's starter **Twice-baked Manx vintage Cheddar cheese soufflé** 90

    Enzo's main course **Rack of Manx lamb, dauphinoise potatoes and port wine jus** 92

    Enzo's dessert **Chocolate and orange cheesecake with cookies ice cream** 95

Titan 96
    Titan's starter **Manx king scallop thermidor** 100
    Titan's main course **Individual beef wellingtons** 102
    Titan's dessert **Chocolate orange deanezze** 104

L'Experience 106
    L'Experience's starter **Steak tartare** 108
    L'Experience's main course **Lobster thermidor served with chips** 110
    L'Experience's dessert **Chocolate Fondant** 113

New Manila 114
    New Manila's starter **Thai lobster salad** 117
    New Manila's main course **Grilled Manx rack of lamb in massaman curry sauce** .. 118
    New Manila's dessert **Thai pandan pancake** 120

Regency Hotel 122
    Regency Hotel's starter **Duo of mackerel** 125
    Regency Hotel's main course **Manx rib of beef** 126
    Regency Hotel's dessert **Manx mess** 128

Seven Kingdom 130
    Seven Kingdom's starter **Kipper pâté on lemon and dill scones with a fennel salad** .. 133
    Seven Kingdom's main course **Seafood gratin** 134
    Seven Kingdom's dessert **Chocolate fondants with mixed fresh berries and vanilla ice cream** .. 137

Portofino 138
    Portofino's starter **Leek and lobster terrine, and pickled cucumber** 141
    Portofino's main course **Crispy braised belly pork, king scallops, curried parsnip purée, pak choi** .. 142
    Portofino's dessert **Chocolate soufflé** 145

Coast 146
    Coast's starter **Manx queenie linguine** 149
    Coast's main course **Herb-crusted chump of Manx lamb with grilled veg and red wine jus** .. 150
    Coast's dessert **Molten toffee pudding** 152

1886 154
    1886's starter **Salmon, Manx crab and Parmesan croquettes with pea shoots** .. 156
    1886's main course **Slow braised local Loaghtan lamb shank in a wild Manx herb crust, beetroot and goat's cheese creamed potatoes** .. 159
    1886's dessert **honeycomb and white chocolate cookie s'mores, with a raspberry, wild berry gin and vanilla cream, topped with a salted caramel sauce** .. 162

Ramsey & the north

Jean-Pierre's Bistro 164
    Jean-Pierre's starter **Twice baked cheese soufflé made with abergavenny mature cheddar** .. 167
    Jean-Pierre's main course **Hay-roasted back saddle of Manx goat** 168
    Jean-Pierre's dessert **Lemon brûlée with homemade shortbread** 170

Contents

Ramsey & the north

Vellika's 172
    Vellika's starter **Chemmeen patties with cassava chips** 175
    Vellika's main course **Jhinja charminar (seabass stuffed with prawns)** 176
    Vellika's dessert **Rice hoppers with ice cream** 179

Milntown 180
    Milntown's starter **Nori rolls** 185
    Milntown's main course **Chicken en croute** 186
    Milntown's dessert **Bombe Alaska** 189

Café Rosa 190
    Café Rosa's starter **Country baked mushrooms (champignons à la campagne)** .. 193
    Café Rosa's main course **Mixed fish platter (fruits de mer)** 194
    Café Rosa's dessert **Rosa's dessert selection (assortiment de petits desserts): profiteroles** 197

Peel & the west

Filbey's 198
    Filbey's starter **Local crab with lobster pâté, pink grapefruit and avocado mousse** 203
    Filbey's main course **Manx pork loin** 204
    Filbey's dessert **Lime and Manx gin posset** 207

The Boatyard 208
    The Boatyard's starter **Queenie pancakes** 211
    The Boatyard's main course **Smoked haddock, leek and pea gratin** 212
    The Boatyard's dessert **Coffee budino** 215

Castletown & the south

The Forge 216
    The Forge's starter **Scallops with hazelnut butter** 219
    The Forge's main course **Blue boy burger** 220
    The Forge's dessert **Brownie** 223

Leonardo's 224
    Leonardo's starter **Classic bouillabaisse** 227
    Leonardo's main course **Tortellini with salmon and ricotta** 228
    Leonardo's dessert **Pears poached in limoncello with crema di latte** 231

The Abbey 232
    The Abbey's starter **Home-smoked salmon and horseradish cream** 235
    The Abbey's main course **Blackened beef fillet** 236
    The Abbey's dessert **Trifle** 239

Eateries

Close Leece Farm Shop and Café 242
    Close Leece's recipe **Close Leece farm chorizo and queenie linguine** 245
Wine Down 246
    Wine Down's recipe **Charcuterie and Artisan Cheese board with crispy bread and fruits**   247
Aaron House 249
    Aaron's House's recipe **Manx ale fruit loaf** 250
The Dovecote Tearoom 251
    The Dovecote's recipe **Cherry and marzipan cake** 252
Secret Pizza 253
    Secret Pizza's recipe **The big cheese** 254
Ticket Hall 256
    Ticket Hall's recipe **Pan-seared locally caught fillet of hake on a bed of cheesy leeks** 258
The Shed 259
    The Shed's recipe **The zest factor!** 261
What the Fork 262
    What the Fork's recipe **The Cypress grill** 263
Versa 264
    Versa's recipe **Wild puffball mushroom, barley, preserved wild garlic and foraged herbs** 265
Tea Junction 266
    Tea Junction's recipe **Honey cloud catcher cake** 267

Distilleries and Wine

Foraging Vintners 270
    Forgaging Vintner's cocktail **Rhugo** 271
Fynoderee 272
Seven Kingdom 274
Bath & Bottle 276
    Bath & Bottle's cocktail **Fynderella** 276

The Island's Pantry 278

Introduction

In 2015 we published the first edition of the *The Island Kitchen*, which was an overwhelming success, selling over 5,000 copies both on the Island and worldwide. The publication proved very successful with all the businesses on the Isle of Man and highlighted the rapidly growing internationally high standard of the restaurants and cafés on offer.

Traditionally known for its excellent kippers, the Island also boasts some of the finest seafood anywhere, including its queenie scallops. With the Island being free from intensive farming methods, the quality of the produce is second to none – Loaghtan sheep provide lamb of the highest quality, while the distinctive taste of the Island's milk and cream is reflected in its award-winning dairy products.

The Island Kitchen illustrates the continued high standard of cuisine that can be found on the Island, showcasing signature dishes from the Isle of Man's finest chefs and restaurants using the abundant, high-quality produce that the Island is renowned for. From succulent starters to delicious desserts, you are sure to find a favourite and keep coming back for more.

In this new edition we have very much followed the same pattern of presentation, and in addition a large number of new businesses have come on board since the last book. The book is divided into five principle chapters: the restaurants, eateries and cafes, distilleries and the Island's pantry, who play an important role for all the organisations with bespoke products. The recipes are varied, imaginative and delicious, whether you are enjoying them at home or eating out, where they will be lovingly created by our Island's skilled chefs. It has been a great pleasure to work with not only each restaurant and café, but also with Robinson's, who play a very important part in the food industry on the Isle of Man. The various government departments on the Isle of Man have been very supportive once again.

My thanks go Simon Park who has worked most of the summer undertaking a vast photography shoot of all the restaurants and cafés all over the Island.

My thanks also to go to our team at Lily Publications, Sara Donaldson, Andrew Lowe, Nicola Green, Emma Ames and Linda Cowsill who have worked very hard to make the publication work as smoothly as possible.

Finally, a word of thanks to my daughter Nicola, who thought of the original concept of the book back in 2015 after leaving university.

Happy cooking and eating.

Miles Cowsill
Managing Editor
October 2019

Robinson's: a provenance in produce

Robinson's, one of the Isle of Man's most well known businesses, is also one of the oldest family businesses on the Island. Starting back in the nineteenth century, with a market stall set up by Mary Robinson, the company has gone from strength to strength and is now in its fifth generation of family management. As a company dedicated to supporting the Island's economy and nurturing local businesses, they know the value of the Island's diverse range of products, and believe that mutual support can help grow the Isle of Man's reputation and put the Island further on the map as a place known for its quality products.

Modest beginnings

In 1886, Mary McGreevy who had married James Robinson in 1871, was looking for a way to earn a little extra income for the family, so she set up a market stall on the North Quay in Douglas, at the 'Fairy Ground'. Over 130 years later, that small market stall has grown in ways she could never have imagined.

Despite a large family of ten, only two lines of the family exist today: four of the children died young; daughter May, who worked in the business died without family; one son, who was a lighthouse keeper, died without issue; another son died at sea, and Mary Ling, a long-time social worker and the last of the other family line, recently passed away. Mary McGreevy's son, Johnny Robinson, expanded the business, moving from the market stall to premises in Nelson Street, and then 30 Strand Street, before moving on to the successful site at number 40 Strand Street. The busy shop was always known as Johnny

Robinson's, so the Robinsons name stuck.

As Johnny had no children, it was his sister, Florence, and her husband Jack Baxter, who carried on trading under the Robinson name. Florence met Jack, a Yorkshireman, after he visited the Island due to his love of the TT races and, despite the interruption of WWI, Jack came back to find Florence and married her soon after. Their daughter, Joan, married Johan Horsthuis, a Dutchman who came to the Island at the end of WWII. When the war ended he returned to the Isle of Man to help Joan's father, and the couple married, taking their part in the business. The family strands now survive in the Horsthuis and Newson families, descended through the female line, via Florence and her sister Margaret respectively.

A family legacy

From Mary Robinson to Johnny and then his sister Florence, the family connections have continued, with Joan passing the business down to her four children, John, Tony, Michael and Peter, with their children now continuing the legacy. A restructure of the board in 2017 led to John Horsthuis being named Chairman, Matty Mathieson-Nelson as Group Operational Director, and Ross Williamson as Retail Director, joining Tony Horsthuis and Noel O'Reilly in the retail arm of the business. Managing Director, Janna Horsthuis, is happy to carry on her great-great-grandmother's tradition of leading the business, in what is very much a family firm.

Originally Robinson's was a mostly retail concern, importing fruit and vegetables once the

Robinson's – established in the 1880's from a market stall at The Old Market Place on Douglas Quay – is now in it's fifth generation as a family business.

market stall moved into dedicated premises. Johnny went to Liverpool to buy produce, which helped the business grow, however he also bought from local farmers. As the shop expanded in Strand Street, the family maintained good relationships between customers, management and staff. Many employees stayed, and still stay, long-term (long-service awards are nothing unusual here) – staff members have always been very much seen as part of the Robinson family.

Modern expansion

Expansion over the years eventually led to the premises Robinson's now occupies: the main depot at Ballapaddag and a shop on Prospect Terrace. The company also has a franchise in all eight Shoprite stores, with a strong alliance with Shoprite's founders, the Nicolson family, which started when Joan and Johan grew their business. What started out as a modest stall in 1886 has become an impressive champion for produce on the Isle of Man, providing the Island and the UK with a wide range of food and floral products. While still a family-run concern, Robinson's now

employs over 175 people and has become a one-stop shop for the Isle of Man's food industry.

A passion for produce
– championing the artisan producers

Having grown from modest beginnings, Robinson's know a thing or two about the pitfalls and struggles of fledgling businesses. Growth is not easy, but can be made easier with help and encouragement from those around you, and the family are committed to helping today's small businesses and artisan producers on the Isle of Man.

Over the past few years the Island has built a strong reputation as a 'foodie' paradise, with new producers moving from kitchen table to small business. With their strong position as a leading supplier, Robinson's are able to encourage those new to the food industry, and are helping connect the ever-growing number of artisan producers with the wider consumer market.

The family are passionate about nurturing emerging businesses and helping them grow. With a strong knowledge of the local community and with expertise in capturing opportunities for scaling micro-businesses, the company builds partnerships with small producers, taking the journey with them into profitable expansion. Nurturing those they work with is beneficial for both businesses and Island alike.

Working with local producers

Paula's Kitchen is one example of a kitchen-table business that has grown beyond its humble beginnings with a little support from Robinson's. Starting out with private orders for her granola, Paula soon started selling at the farmers' market and the IOM Food Assembly, then supplied her products through the Good Health Store in Port Erin. Soon Paula moved to a larger kitchen and after meeting with Robinson's she began to supply The Terrace with her range. A pop-up tasting led to more orders, and Robinson's have been happy to help promote her brand. All Paula's Kitchen

products are gluten, dairy, additive and refined sugar-free, and she now has a large corporate client base as well as supplying many of the Island's delicatessens and cafés, as well as Robinson's themselves.

The Dairy Shed couldn't be more different, as indicated by their name. Bill and Kirree Callow show that nurtured herds produce exceptional dairy products. The milk from their herd of Ayrshire cows, the only such herd on the Island, is turned into yoghurt that is produced and packaged entirely on-site. Starting off with Kirree experimenting as a means of diversification, the small batches of yoghurt given to family and friends quickly led to attending the Isle of Man Food and Drink Festival and meeting potential customers. The family soon started to stock local stores and attended more shows before making the move to produce full-time. Meeting with Dave and Paul from Robinson's led to their brand being

stocked in The Terrace, and being championed and bought by their loyal customer base, all of whom are more than happy to buy a local product made using home-grown produce.

Robinson's and The Isle of Man Creamery have been working closely together for over thirty years to support local farmers, helping to create a sustainable economy for the Island's producers and helping ensure their long-term economic stability. The creamery is a farmer-owned cooperative involving thirty-three of the Island's farms, ranging from small to large herds, all adhering to strict standards: only the best, freshest milk and cream is passed on to the consumer. Isle of Man cows benefit from long outdoor grazing on lush pastures, being grass-fed for an average of 203 days of the year, which leads to a milk that is known for its consistent high quality, and this in turn leads to excellent cream, cheese and butter. Add to that the extremely low mileage between the farms, the creamery and Robinson's, and it's good news all round – whether buying dairy products from Robinson's outlets, buying wholesale from the

depot or being part of the catering service, customers know they are helping the Island's farmers and its economy.

Another long-term collaboration Robinson's has is with Davison's ice-cream. For over twenty-five years the two companies have been working closely together to supply the Island with quality ice cream and chocolates. Originally starting out in 1988, making handmade confectionary, the family soon moved into creating delicious ice cream using only Manx butter, cream and milk and locally sourced produce. The Davisons believe in collaboration and quality as a path to success and continued growth as a family business, and working closely with Robinson's has helped to expand their reach beyond their own premises in Peel. Since collaborating with Robinson's in the food services arm of the business, Davison's have scaled up in impressive ways. As well as being a firm family favourite, with local customers and tourists regularly visiting the ice cream parlour for a treat, the company supplies Robinson's retail and wholesale, and they supply the food services division with a huge amount of ice cream – roughly 40,000 litres a year! This is all down to a shared vision for reliable quality, investment in the business and their community, and good old fashioned hard work with excellent customer service.

But it's not all sweet treats and produce that are supplied by Robinson's. Ramsey Bakery has joined forces with them to provide Isle of Man residents with their daily bread. A long-established family firm, the bakery has been supplying the Island since 1972 and is now the Isle of Man's leading bakery, supplying all food retailers with their bread products each morning. As with any viable business, it wasn't an easy road to expansion, but perseverance and a quality product led to the bakery surviving and thriving. The late 1980s and early 90s saw massive investment, which doubled the size of the business, and the quality and consistency of their products are a testament to their workforce who, like Robinson's, are not unknown to reach long service. Ramsey Bakery is another business who believes in community cooperation, and the flour they use amounts to over 90% of the Laxey Glen Mill's production. When consumers buy their Ramsey Bakery bread and rolls from Robinson's they can be assured that they are buying a quality product, made from Manx wheat by a family company who believe in supplying their customers with the freshest products of a consistently high standard.

Staarvey Farm herbs, micro salad and organic salad leaves are regularly found in top restaurants as well as cafés, pubs and homes throughout the Isle of Man. Supplying quality seasonal products is a passion for the Devereaus, passed on perhaps by Stephen's grandfather who was the first market gardener to commercially grow courgettes in the 1960s – selling his produce in Covent Garden and being mentioned in the books of the influential cookery writer, Elizabeth David. All Staarvey Farm leaves and vegetables are grown organically, without chemicals or pesticides, picked daily, and chilled and bagged or boxed on site. Despite also running a free-range egg business, the family decided to concentrate on their growing, and closed down the egg business in 2015, not an easy decision but the right one judging from the every-growing popularity of their produce. Scaling up often means concentrating on one aspect of the business, and now the family are winning awards and reaching more customers with their products being available through Robinson's. When their seasonal leaves are not available the Devereaus create a wide range of preserves, cordials, sauces and dressings, available year-round.

Being the Isle of Man's leading fresh produce supplier, Robinson's source their produce locally wherever possible, and are committed to supporting Manx farmers and growers. They have a long-term relationship with Allanson's, the largest vegetable producer on the Island, stocking their seasonal produce, including a large range of root vegetables, cabbages and rhubarb, and helping them reach more of the Island's population. Understanding their suppliers' and customers' needs is paramount to Robinson's success, and as part of their food services aspect of the business, suppliers such as Allanson's have scaled up to help supply local hospitals, schools and hotels as well as the Island's restaurants and cafés.

Ballanelson, a small commercial nursery in Jurby run by Robert and Gill Kneale, supplies Robinson's with tomatoes and strawberries. Chances are, if you've bought local strawberries or tomatoes, they were grown here. Another long-established family business, they also make chutneys and honey as well as growing domestic plants. When the food miles are this low you can be guaranteed your soft fruits will reach you in the best possible condition.

As Robinson's keep an eye on what's new on the market, it's only fitting that they help to nurture what is perhaps the Island's most unusual food brand. James Callow's experimentation with growing crops on his sheep and beef farm at Bride, Maughold and St Mark's, has led to Isle of Man Quinoa. A delicious crop that you wouldn't normally expect to be grown here.

Ensuring Quality

Retail food services and flowers are at the heart of Robinson's business today, but it's not just local produce that appears, with two World Food Market outlets helping to cater for the growth in Thai, Chinese, Philippine and Indian cuisine over the last ten years. The company also hold a franchise for fruit and vegetables in all Shoprite and Iceland stores across the Island. Robinson's are proud to serve a diverse range of customers, from members of the public wanting to buy the best local produce, to restauranteurs ensuring only the finest, freshest ingredients for their dishes.

The Fish Market, established in 2015, allows Robinson's to collaborate with the Island's fish and seafood suppliers, bringing the freshest local fish and seafood, for which the Isle of Man is renowned, directly to both restauranteurs and consumers. Horne Seafood (C.B. Horne Ltd), the oldest seafood processing business on the Isle of Man, supplies the Island's famous king and queen scallops and crabmeat. After taking over the

business from his father, Barry, Simon Horne is now at the helm, and as well as supplying the UK and Europe with this special Manx delicacy, he is committed to making sure the scallops eaten on the Isle of Man are caught by Manx fishermen and of the highest possible quality. Both Horne Seafood and Robinson's believe in supporting the Island economy and supplying value and quality to all their customers, whether that be the individual looking for a few pieces for supper, or a top-class establishment looking to buy in bulk. Supplying the Island's residents, restaurants, cafés and pubs, with the help of Robinson's, ensures that the Islanders get their pick of the highest quality Manx produce. Robinson's themselves have also expanded into producing their own special-recipe smoked salmon, which can be delivered via the Royal Mail to addresses throughout the Isle of Man and the UK.

Food Services

Due to Robinson's passion for helping local businesses, and over a hundred years of retail knowledge, they have a knack for helping small suppliers grow. Starting off as a small family business, to where they are now, with a 50,000 sq ft depot and distribution centre as well as retail space, the company supplies over 10,000 different product lines to over 90% of business, schools, hospitals and caterers throughout the Isle of Man.

They understand that small family businesses can grow if given the opportunity and plenty of encouragement. By listening to what producers aim to achieve through their business goals, and through solid partnerships, Robinson's can help small suppliers take the first steps towards growing their business.

A number of household names on the Isle of Man have taken just that journey and work closely with Robinson's in the food services side of the business. Operating along with Robinson's, Davison's, Ramsey Bakery and the Isle of Man Creamery help provide both public and private

sector establishments with their high quality products. Through the company's expertise in distribution and sourcing quality brands, smaller companies or producers can become more cost effective by utilising Robinson's supplier knowledge. The food services part of the company is a huge undertaking, but those brands who decide to take this route are nurtured and helped to grow, with Robinson's being with them every step of the way. With such high quality products being produced on the Isle of Man, the opportunity for small and family businesses to expand and achieve viable growth is a very real prospect. Robinson's can see the potential in Island producers and want to encourage more people to take their business to the next level.

From Family to Community

As part of their commitment to the community, Robinson's reaches every primary school on the Island, regularly visiting schools with their mascots, Mr Chunks (a giant Pineapple) and Mrs Smoothie (a giant Strawberry). They talk to the children about healthy eating and the 5-a-day ideal, and through their ethos of encouragement and nurturing, they educate through talks about local and worldwide produce. As the pupils learn about fruits and vegetables they know, and some they don't, the benefits of a healthy lifestyle are taught. But it's not all educational, there's lots of fun to be had with competitions and projects to take part in.

The family also give their support to the popular Chef of the Year and Student Chef of the Year competitions. Championing the upcoming generations of chefs, who will in their turn use the quality produce grown on the Isle of Man, is an important way of highlighting the importance of sustainable living.

Environmental and recycling projects, for example through their recycling of packaging, composting organic waste and reduced energy consumption, are also important to Robinson's in a bid to help lower their impact on the Island.

Buying local, of course, is an important way in which customers on the Isle of Man help reduce air and travel miles, and with Robinson's committed to local producers and businesses, they can easily find what they are looking for, and have a positive impact on both the environment and the Island's economy.

Moving Forward in the C21st

Life has definitely changed since Mary Robinson's time. New technologies have made life easier, we're connected to the world in a way we once never thought possible and communication is instantaneous.

Robinson's new systems are helping to make this growing business more efficient than ever before. The recent £300,000 investment in an IT system and picking technology has increase the pick efficiency at the distribution centre from 80% to 97.9%.

The once small family business is now a major employer on the Isle of Man. Robinson's may employ over 175 people, but it's still very much a family firm, with each and every employee thought of as a member of the Robinson's family. Long-service awards are still very much a part of life.

It would be difficult to include every supplier involved with the company, however a few are listed below. After 133 years our mission is still to serve the freshest produce and flowers at the best value with superb customer service.

Our local producers and suppliers include:
Allanson's Farm, Ramsey Bakery, Laxey Glen Flour Mills, Staarvey Farms, Ellerslie Rapeseed Oil, David Kneale, Roly's Chocolate, Mann Speciality Foods, Isle of Man Creamery, A&J Butchers, Andreas Meat Co., Leela's Kitchen, Isle of Man Quinoa, Finnans Eggs, Noa Bakehouse, Davisons Ice Cream, Mike Kneale, Robert & Gill Kneale at Ballanelson Nurseries, Les Kneale, Morris Cooil and Paddy's Hooked on Fish.

Isle of Man food & drink

The Isle of Man is a very special destination. It's the only entire country in the world to have been awarded UNESCO Biosphere status, recognising the way its people and culture harmonise with nature and the stunning landscapes that surround them.

In biosphere regions, conservation encompasses the idea of creating and maintaining the very best environment and community to provide for us – our water, our health, our well-being.

The rich tapestry of the Island's agriculture is interwoven into this ideal and it is against this backdrop that passionate food and drink entrepreneurs are using the raw ingredients the Island's farmers, growers and fishermen produce to create a wide range of award-winning products and great places to eat. In turn, people on the Island are increasingly seeking out, and taking a pride in, food which they know has been produced sensitively and sustainably.

Close Leece Farm

It is, of course, not the only Island in the British Isles that can proudly boast its own 'heirloom' foods. Jersey for example, has delicious new potatoes and rich milk from its indigenous cows.

But just to put it into context: the Isle of Man is nearly five times the size of Jersey, with a smaller population. At 572 square kilometres (221 square miles), the Isle of Man is also larger than the Isle of Wight and nearly ten times the size of Guernsey.

The Isle of Man has the wide-open space that Jersey and the other Channel Islands lack, and a great deal of that space is occupied, in one form or another, by agriculture. And, despite being further north, its comparatively frost-free climate not only allows palm trees to flourish (the Isle of Man has its own indigenous palm tree) but also helps the local growers and provides rich pastures for its livestock. About 85 per cent of the Isle of Man is given over to agricultural production, with

about 450 farms, and you will see the signs of this everywhere as you drive around.

Whether it is sheep grazing on the purple heather hillsides, cows chewing the cud in lush green pastures, or free-range hens clucking by the side of narrow lanes, this is an Island with a big investment, both emotionally and financially, in farming, growing and producing.

Local people love to get out and around the Island, walking and cycling the footpaths and greenways. They see the farming and growing process at first hand and feel close to it and they appreciate that farmers are the guardians of our rich and varied landscape.

In a small community like the Isle of Man, if you buy local food it is very easy to trace it right back to its roots.

One way to be sure that food is local is to look out for the 'Isle of Man Provenance' label, indicating that it has been grown, reared, caught and/or processed in the Isle of Man and/or contains mostly Manx ingredients.

Manx dairy products are a great example of traceability.

All the milk, butter and cheese carrying the **Isle of Man Creamery** brand can be traced back to just 33 farms, all within 18 miles of the creamery.

'The milk tastes better here,' a visitor to the Island told me recently.

That's not surprising: all 25 million litres of milk collected from the farms is accredited under a government 'grass fed' scheme which ensures the highest standards of nutrition and animal welfare in the British Isles.

'It is the most robust and thoroughly audited scheme in the dairy industry,' says creamery managing director, Findlay Macleod.

It's good for the farmers, too, as they tend to be on higher-paid contracts than some of their counterparts in the British Isles.

Around seven million litres of the milk the creamery takes in will be sold on the Island as liquid milk. The remainder goes into cheese, with excess cream being processed into butter or sold as cream.

The big success story has been the Isle of Man Creamery's range of cheeses, and winners of numerous industry awards. The history of cheesemaking on the Isle of Man can be traced back to Viking times, and its cheesemaking today reflects those traditional skills.

Of the 1,400 tonnes of cheese made each year, 300 tonnes are sold on the Island and the rest is exported to the UK, the US, Malta, the Middle East, and Ireland.

'The provenance is a crucial part of our selling story in terms of the location and the heritage of the Island – it's a great story,' explains Findlay Macleod, managing director of the creamery.

There are also two small, single-farm dairies on the Island: **Aalin Dairy** and **Cooil Brothers**.

Carl Huxham's herd of dairy cows at Cronk Aalin Farm in Sulby graze on rich pasture 5,000 feet above sea level and drink water from a spring. Carl and his wife, Sarah, have turned old cattle sheds into a state-of-the-art dairy where he bottles his milk in traditional one-pint bottles with foil tops.

Cooil Brothers' 100 milking cows graze the lush pastures of the family farm in Port Erin.

They provide fresh Manx milk and cream, which is bottled and delivered direct to customers in recyclable bottles.

And, if you want to know exactly where your yoghurt has come from, look out for **'The Dairy Shed'** brand in local shops. It is all made on a family farm in Andreas from the milk supplied by their herd of Ayrshire cows. All stages from production to packaging take place on the farm and the only food miles incurred are at the delivery stage.

They make plain and some imaginatively flavoured yoghurts – think gingerbread, and coconut and lime – and their products have won multiple Great Taste awards.

For goat's cheese fans, **Isle of Man Goats**, in Kirk Michael, run a herd of Anglo-Nubian goats, renowned for their milk-producing capabilities. They produce soft cheeses and two styles of feta,

creamy and crumbly, in their purpose-built cheese room and they also run a farm café.

With all this wealth of dairy products you'd expect the ice cream on the Isle of Man to be good, and it is. **Davison's and Manx Ices** are available at outlets around the Island and offer dairy-free and diabetic options.

Because the majority of livestock is slaughtered on the Island, rather than being shipped to meat plants in the UK, Manx meat is also a totally traceable product. You will often find a board in the local butcher's shop indicating the names of the farms their meat has come from that week.

Most of it is marketed through **Isle of Man Meats**, which runs the meat plant. They work with 202 Manx farms to produce the very best local beef, lamb and pork. The company prides itself on knowing all these farmers personally, which underpins exceptional quality right the way through from pasture to plate.

This relationship has become even closer with the appointment of one of the most experienced and well-qualified young farmers on the Island, Kirree Kermode, as its procurement officer.

Kirree says: 'Sheep are my passion and the most important part of my role is to be in contact with farmers, showing what the plant needs for their animals to reach the right specifications for Isle of Man Meats.

'The Island's agricultural industry produces some of the finest quality beef, lamb and pork available, and has an excellent record and reputation for raising livestock to the highest standards.'

You will find Isle of Man meat in butchers and supermarkets all around the Island.

Andreas Meat Company, based in the north of the Island, takes between 80–90 per cent of the pork from Isle of Man Meats to make a range of high-quality sausages and burgers, also sold in **Shoprite** stores and other outlets around the Island under their own brand and the **Ballacushag** brand. In 2018 our products won six Great Taste awards; we believe that great tasting, quality Manx produce can be affordable for everyone.

Manx pork is also used to make **Dave's Delicious Dogs**, a hot dog company founded by American ex-pat Dave Valkema after he realised you couldn't buy a really authentic hot dog on the Island. Now you can and you will find them at the **Ramsey Delicatessen** and **Soup Pot**.

Five generations of the Teare family have farmed at **Ballakelly Farm**, in the north of the Island. The latest incumbents, Alan Teare, his wife Rachel and their two children, raise pigs, beef cattle and sheep and sell their meat direct to customers through their own butchery and farm shop. Many of their products, including their pork shoulder, sausages and burgers, have won UK Great Taste awards.

Another local meat company, **Close Leece Farm** has also won numerous Great Taste awards for its charcuterie, including the highest accolade, the three-star award, signifying a product the judges described as 'exquisite,' for its Manx Chorizo.

All Close Leece charcuterie is made with pork from the farm's rare breed Tamworth pigs, except for one unusual salami which is made with Manx Loaghtan lamb.

Loaghtans are the Island's indigenous sheep breed. 'Loaghtan' is Manx for 'mouse,' referring to their mouse-brown colour. They are a slow-growing breed, producing meat which is darker in colour and much leaner than the more commercial breeds. It is especially well-suited to making burgers and it's worth looking out for these on the menus of a number of eateries on the Island.

Ballakarran Meat Company specialises in pasture-fed lamb and beef but also supplies a wide range of local food products, making it a one-stop shop for local meat and produce. Look out for their distinctive van at locations around the Island.

Whilst it frequently causes logistical problems for farmers and food producers, the Island's geographical isolation has also worked in its favour: the Island boasts a bee population free from the ravages of the varroa mite, thanks to strict import controls; no foxes means that our hens can range free, safely (though we do have a small polecat population), and in 2001 the Island took drastic measures (including cancelling its iconic TT Races) that successfully prevented the foot and mouth outbreak spreading from the UK to our shores.

The logistical problems mean that if the weather is too bad the boat bringing imported foods to the Island cannot sail. This encourages more reliance on home-produced food and nowhere more so than in the production of flour and bread.

Most of the arable farming takes place in the north of the Island and there is a close relationship between the farmers, the Island's flour mill and local bakeries.

Around a dozen farmers grow wheat each year according to the requirements of the Island's flour mill, **Laxey Glen Mills**, making the flour they produce completely traceable.

Regulations governing the production of flour in the UK require a number of additional ingredients, such as calcium carbonate and iron be added to flour. No such regulations exist in the Island, making the flour uniquely pure.

The Island's biggest bakery, **Ramsey Bakery**, is their largest customer: their bread is sold in supermarkets and convenience stores all over the Island.

There are also a number of smaller, artisan bakeries, including **Noa Bakehouse** and **Ross Bakery**.

Noa makes classic sourdough bread, everyday sliced tin loaves, and award-winning rye bread. Owner Miles Pettit has been a passionate supporter of Laxey Glen Mills and local farmers. When he found that rye flour was the only type of flour he needed to import for his loaves he worked closely with one local arable farmer and the mill to produce a Manx rye flour, which he now uses.

In addition to wheat and rye, there is now a movement to return to growing a crop that was once seen all over the Island: oats. The growing popularity of porridge, oat cereal bars and vegan products such as oat milk has increased the demand for oats across the UK and Europe.

The Riggall family at **Great Meadow Estate** in Castletown have converted their 150 acres to organic, mostly down to oats, and encouraged other farmers to try it too. They have built a silo where they can store both organically grown and non-organic oats separately and, as they don't store any wheat or other grains, their oats are guaranteed to be gluten-free.

If you like granola for breakfast you'll love the luxury range from **Paula's Kitchen** which uses locally grown ingredients wherever possible and features flavours like Summer Strawberry, Almond and Chia. It's also gluten, refined sugar, dairy and additive free.

Breaking new ground, James Callow, who runs an 840-acre sheep and beef farm spread over land at Bride, Maughold and St Mark's, decided to experiment with growing quinoa and it has been a great success, now sold as **Isle of Man Quinoa**.

Of course, living on an Island, you never forget about the riches from the seas around our coastline.

The Isle of Man, backed by specific scientific research, was an early adopter of sustainable fishing practices.

'The Isle of Man fishing industry started its conservation practices many years ago in the late 1970s,' says William Caley, manager of **Isle of Man Seafood Products Ltd**. 'The UK only has one per cent of its waters under protection, whereas nearly half of Manx waters have protection measures.'

Isle of Man Seafood Products has a fleet of seven boats fishing for queenies (Manx queen scallops). Like all the Manx fishing fleets they fish only with nets, rather than dredge gear, which damages the sea bed by bringing everything along in its wake.

Queenies are so popular on the Island they have been voted the official Manx National Dish,

flash-fried with a good measure of garlic and bacon. You will find some version of a queenie dish on menus in most of the Island's restaurants. A queenie bap is another local delicacy not to be missed.

If you want to try cooking them yourself you'll find all the freshest seafood ingredients, including queenies, at **Robinson's Fish Market** in Braddan and **The Fish House** in Port St Mary.

Historically, the fish of choice for Manx people – and one of their diet staples – was the herring. The reason for this was simple: these fish ran in shoals and so were easy to catch in great numbers. In the days before refrigeration, these oily fish, unlike fresh white fish, could be salted down and stored through the winter. Then, in the 1830s, another method of preserving was discovered – smoking – and the famous Manx kipper was born.

There are some great vegetable growers on the

Island and **Robinson's**, the Island's premier greengrocers, support these local growers wherever possible. They have their own shops and also supply **Shoprite** supermarkets around the Island.

For one of their suppliers, **Staarvey Farm**, growing great veggies and salads is in the genes. Owner Stephen Devereau remembers his grandfather's market garden in Surrey where the first courgettes were grown, back in the 1960s. In those days, they were all snapped up by expensive restaurants in London. Now he and his wife, Jenny, grow organic salads and herbs and make a wide range of preserves. They also supply local restaurants and their soft fruit is used in cocktails at the popular **Bath & Bottle** in Douglas.

Which brings us nicely onto the subject of drinks and the Island has several noteworthy drinks producers.

Will Faulds and Charlotte Traynor run the **Apple Orphanage**, just outside Peel. They make a range of single-variety apple juices, fruit pressés, Manx dry cider and Keshal (a Manx elderflower fizz) from fruits they grow themselves or acquire via their fruit exchange. 'If anyone has any excess fruit they can pick it when it's nice and ripe and bring it to us. We will weigh it and then let them choose some of our drinks to take away in exchange,' explains Charlotte.

For something a bit more intoxicating, the Isle of Man also has three distilleries, **Seven Kingdom** in Douglas, and **Fynoderee** and **Glen Kella**, based in the north of the Island.

Glen Kella produces Manx Spirit, which is colourless but with the taste and aroma of whisky.

Seven Kingdom is a small distillery, which specialises in ultra-smooth, delicate, balanced, spirits, notably gin and vodka. Their spirits are produced using a 150l German copper pot still made by the Kothe factory in Eislingen.

Fynoderee uses a character from Manx folklore in its stylish branding. They produce a range of gins, one for each season, and a vodka with 'a tiny touch' of Manx honey.

Not surprisingly in a small community, Manx food and drink producers frequently meet, and this can lead to collaborations including one which has seen Fynoderee produce their Kerala Chai Edition, one of the first gins to ever be created specifically for pairing with Indian and Asian cuisine.

For this they worked with Kumar Menon, a long-time Island resident who imports and blends spices from his native Kerala in India, and who works with **Teare's butchers** in Ramsey supplying spice marinades for their meats.

Foraging Vintners is a small wine bar and craft winery, set in a stunning location overlooking Port Erin Bay, producing non-grape-based varieties of sparkling wine. You sit outside on their terrace on a summer's day and enjoy a glass of their own elderflower and rhubarb sparkling wines, on their own or used in a range of cocktails.

The Isle of Man also has a growing street food movement.

Betty Pie Co. runs a pie van, stocked with delicious, handmade pies packed with Manx ingredients like steak and ale, Loaghtan lamb and macaroni cheese. Vicky Quirk, who runs the van, makes all the pies herself – around 300 a week.

What The Fork offers global street-food event catering, using local meat and produce. They have a variety of menus to suit every occasion, from tacos and quesadillas, to carved Manx meats on oven-baked ciabattas and Mediterranean mezze-style cuisine.

Look out for **Black Dog Pizza Oven** at events like Bushy's TT Village and the Isle of Man Food and Drink Festival. They produce an amazing range of pizzas from a traditional pizza oven in a converted horse trailer. They typically prove their dough for two days and use local and foraged ingredients for their toppings, including Manx queenies and chorizo and wild garlic pesto.

The **Secret Pizza Company** also started out as a pop-up street food van but has now found a permanent home in Castletown. They make a range of hand-crafted pizzas with vegetarian and vegan toppings including pulled jackfruit. They

The Childrens Centre grown Cucumbers 50p

have also collaborated with the **Cow & Pig Smokehouse**, who provides toppings like pulled pork for their pizzas.

Cow & Pig Smokehouse was started by Harry Davies who bought and renovated an old trailer and kitted it out with a giant American smoking oven to turn it into a touring smokehouse.

When you consider all the vast range of quality local food and drink available on the Island, it's clear that this didn't all happen by accident.

The inherent loyalty of the Manx public to locally grown and produced products, and the growing acknowledgement of their quality, led to them being given the backing of official government strategy.

'Food Matters' represents the formalising of support for the Island's increasingly entrepreneurial farmers, fishermen, growers, producers and others in the local food and drink industry. It is a recognition of the value of the food industry in the local economy and its potential for growth.

Geoffrey Boot MHK, Minister for Environment, Food and Agriculture says: 'As an Island we are extremely proud of our food industry and are looking to grow and support the industry through the Isle of Man Government's Food Matters strategy.

'We are fortunate to have a number of leading food and drink producers who are helping us make a significant name for ourselves both on the Isle of Man and internationally too. With a wealth of fantastic local products and ingredients we're able to create delicious, local, award-winning food and drink that can be enjoyed throughout the year.

Julie Blackburn

14 North

14 North Quay, Douglas IM1 4LE
01624 664414
www.14north.im

Part of the Rock Food Concepts group, 14 North opened its doors in August 2010 with the aim of showcasing the finest produce the Isle of Man's farmers and artisanal suppliers have to offer. Though a few things have changed since we first launched, our commitment to seasonal, fresh and locally sourced produce remains our biggest driving force – for everyone, from our kitchen team through to our head chef and our friendly and welcoming front of house staff.

We are located on Douglas' North Quay in a beautiful old Manx building that has been redesigned using wood and brick to provide a laid back setting for any event; whether a business lunch, candlelit date night or a celebratory meal with friends.

We always strive to provide the warmest possible welcome and genuine hospitality, no matter what the occasion.

The food scene on the Island continues to go from strength to strength and we have a bigger selection than ever of local food and drink options, new eateries and passionate producers; a scene we are proud to be part of.

Starter from 14 North

King scallop ceviche with puffed roe crackers, toasted sunflower
seeds, avocado and wasabi purée, pickled watermelon, lemon rind, radish and shiso
serves 6

This dish is a perfect way to enjoy the sweetness of our beautiful local scallops, and to showcase how well they pair with many different ingredients, such as watermelon, while also trying to utilise the whole scallop, including the roe. The most important part of this dish is to source the best possible scallops available, preferably still live then prepared and blast frozen before being safe to eat raw.

Ingredients

12 large king scallops

Scallop Marinade

zest and juice of 2 limes
30g light soy
25g rice vinegar
20g mirin (rice wine similar to sake, lower alcohol, higher sugar)
10g Manx honey
10g wasabi (reduce quantity if desired for a lower level of spice)
10ml neutral oil (we use a light pomace)

Puffed Roe Crackers

50g cleaned scallop roe (trim and use only orange part)
100g tapioca starch
100g intense fish stock
5g katsuobushi flakes (other dried smoked fish equivalent would suffice)
salt and cayenne pepper to taste

Sunflower Seeds

60g sunflower seeds
coarse sea salt

Avocado and Wasabi Purée

4 perfectly ripe avocadoes
juice of 2 limes
1 tsp wasabi paste
50ml water
table salt to taste

Lemon Rind Purée

6 large lemons
100g sugar syrup
3 tbsp extra virgin olive oil

Watermelon Pickle

100g white wine vinegar
50g caster sugar
50g raspberry juice (we use raspberry consommé made by cooking raspberries over a bain-marie for 2 hours and then hanging overnight).
10 pink peppercorns
2 bay leaves
half a ripe watermelon

Garnish

sliced radish
micro red shiso
green leaf shiso

Method

For the Scallop Marinade

Zest the limes then finely chop the zest, juice the flesh and combine with the remaining ingredients.

For the Puffed Roe Crackers

First clean the scallops for the main dish and reserve the white meat for later. Wash the roe thoroughly and trim to use only the orange part, discarding the rest. Blend the orange roe in a food processor for no longer than 10 seconds and pass through a fine sieve. Next mix the roe paste with 75g of the tapioca starch to make a kind of dough, cover and leave to one side.

Bring the fish stock to 90°C and leave to stand with the salt, cayenne and dried fish flakes added to infuse for 5–6 minutes, drop the temperature to 70°C and then strain.

Mix in all of the warm stock with the roe and tapioca dough, stirring until it is fully incorporated.

Dust the remains of the tapioca starch onto a flat surface and roll the dough into a long sausage shape (if too wet to handle add a touch more tapioca), roll well in cling film and tie each end.

Steam the roll for one hour and then chill.

(continued on page 30)

King scallop ceviche

Preheat oven to 60°C / gas ¼

Once cold, cut the log into segments the thickness of a one-pound coin, place on a non-stick tray lined with greaseproof paper with a touch of oil, and bake at 60°C for 6–7 hours until completely crisp and transparent.

Deep fry at 180°C. Within 2–3 seconds the crackers will treble in size and puff. Drain on kitchen towel and season with salt (the dry crackers will keep in an airtight container for no longer than 2 days).

For the Sunflower Seeds

Preheat oven to 160°C / gas 3

Simply toast whole seeds in an oven at 160°C for around 6–8 minutes or toast in a pan until golden brown. While warm grind with a mortar and pestle, with a pinch of coarse sea salt, until lightly broken down.

For the Avocado and Wasabi Purée

Clean the avocado flesh into a bowl. Juice the limes on top and then season with salt and break down with a fork. Next put all the ingredients, including the avocado mixture, into a food processor and blend until smooth, for no longer than one minute to prevent the mixture from going brown. Add more water if required, then pass through a small sieve.

For the Lemon Rind Purée

Halve the lemons, juice and deseed. Leave the juice to one side.

Bring the juiced lemons to boil in cold water and then drain the water (repeat 6–7 times until the water is no longer bitter).

Add the lemon rinds (which should be soft) back to the pan with the sugar syrup and boil for 30 seconds. While warm, blend until smooth with the olive oil and the juice from the lemons (add more sugar or lemon juice as desired).

For the Watermelon Pickle

In a pan, bring the vinegar and sugar to the boil, add the raspberry juice, peppercorns and bay leaves and allow to chill.

Cut the watermelon to your desired shape (we use a medium Parisian scoop, and with the trimmings we make a watermelon sorbet for one of our desserts).

Drop the watermelon in the pickle and sous vide (if making at home leave in the liquid in the fridge overnight to allow the watermelon to absorb the pickle).

To Serve

Cut the cleaned scallops into 2 or 3 pieces widthways depending on size and submerge in the marinade for 4–5 minutes.

While the scallops are marinating, spoon roughly 1 tablespoon of toasted sunflower seeds into the centre of each plate, then add 6–7 pieces of watermelon per plate, drained and randomly scattered.

Next add 3 to 4 small teaspoons of avocado purée and lemon purée, placed randomly.

Remove the scallops from the marinade, drain and place on each plate filling in the gaps.

Add sliced radish and shiso as desired.

Finally add the deep-fried roe puffs and season to taste.

Main course from 14 North

Pan-seared Gressingham duck breast

and confit leg, with braised fennel, poached peach, peach and grapefruit gel, amaretti biscuits and corriander oil, beurre noisette powder and amaretto jus

serves 6–8

   This dish allows us to utilise most of the whole duck, serving both the breasts and the legs as well as using the carcasses to make the jus. Duck is very versatile, pairing well with sweet and sour ingredients and aniseed flavours, which are the main components of the dish. We only use Gressingham duck as it has a good balance between a gamey mallard and a more meaty Pekin.. *(continued on page 32)*

Pan-seared Gressingham duck breast

Ingredients

For the Duck

2 whole ducks
1 ltr brine (we use 10% table salt, 10% caster sugar, 80% filtered water)
1 cup of salt/sugar cure (we use 2 parts demerara sugar to 1 part table salt)

Braised Fennel

10 peppercorns
4 bay leaves
2 ltr full-fat milk
2 fennel bulbs
salt and white pepper

Poached Peach

4 ripe peaches
200g white wine vinegar
100g caster sugar
25ml grenadine

Peach and Grapefruit Gel

2 large pink grapefruit
2 ripe peaches
50g caster sugar
5g gellan gum type f (optional)
lemon juice (optional)

Amaretti Biscuit

250g caster sugar
50g ground almonds
75g peeled hazelnuts
2 drops of bitter almond essence
60g egg whites

Beurre Noisette Powder

200g butter
150g maltose
salt and pepper to taste

Coriander Oil

100g coriander leaf
150g pomace olive oil

Amaretto and Duck Jus

2 beef tomatoes
2 garlic cloves
1 onion
1 celery stick
½ fennel bulb
1 tbsp tomato purée
200ml white wine
500g roasted duck bones (reserved from the carcasses)
10 white peppercorns
2 bay leaves
2 ltr water
dash of Amaretto

Method

For the Duck

Remove the breast meat and legs from the carcasses and keep separate. You may ask your butcher to do this for you. Next remove the thigh bones, setting these aside, and submerge the legs in cold brine for a minimum of 4 hours (but for best results, overnight).

Score the skin of the breasts, removing any unwanted sinew, then submerge the breasts in the salt/sugar cure for 1 hour, or longer if using a larger duck breast.

Roast the thigh bones, breast trimmings and carcasses on a medium heat until golden brown, then set aside for creating the amaretto and duck jus. When brined and cured, wash the duck thoroughly under cold water and pat dry.

If cooking at home without sous vide equipment, preheat oven to 120°C / gas ½ for the legs and 180°C / gas 4 for the breasts.

Place the duck legs in a roasting tray with a cup-full of water and braise at 120°C for 2 hours.

Once the water has fully evaporated turn up the temperature on the oven for 20 minutes and allow the skin to crisp.

Place the breast skin side down in a cold pan and over a low heat. Allow the fat to render before turning up the heat to crisp the skin. Then finish in an oven set to 180°C until the internal temperature reaches 49°C and rest for 10 minutes before carving.

Chef's note: *We sous vide and water bath the duck legs and breasts at different times and temperatures to obtain maximum results:*

For the legs sous vide overnight at 75°C. Once cooked, press the leg under a weight and chill to ensure a clean presentation. For the breast meat, sous vide for one hour at 64°C and chill.

For the Braised Fennel

Preheat oven to 160°C/gas 3

Place a tablespoon of water in a heavy-bottomed saucepan with the peppercorns and bay leaves. Add the milk, increasing the temperature until it almost boils. Cut the fennel into wedges and submerge in the hot milk. Braise for 1 hour in 160°C oven or until soft, test using a sharp knife. Season to taste.

For the Poached Peach

Peel the peaches, cut in half and remove the stones. Next boil the vinegar and sugar together to make a pickling liquid *(continued on page 34)*

Pan-seared Gressingham duck breast

and add the grenadine along with the peaches. Simmer on a low heat for around 15 minutes or until soft.

For the Peach and Grapefruit Gel

Juice the grapefruit into a non-metallic bowl. Destone the peaches and blend them whole before squeezing through a cheesecloth into the grapefruit juice. Next, in a saucepan, heat the juice and sugar to 90°C, then add the gellan gum and whisk vigorously. Chill.

Once set, re-blend the gel until it becomes a smooth, fluid gel. Adjust to taste with a squeeze of lemon or sugar, depending on personal preference.

Chef's note: *If at home, you may pass the peaches through a sieve instead of a cheesecloth. This produces a more viscous consistency and therefore you can skip the gellan gum step. At the restaurant we prefer the smoother texture given from the added step.*

For the Amaretti Biscuit

Preheat oven to 160°C/gas 3

Blend the sugar and nuts to a paste, then fold in the bitter almond essence and egg whites. Pipe the mixture onto a lightly floured tray and rest for 8 hours and allow to form a crust.

Bake at 160°C for 10 minutes or until golden brown. Use the same day.

For the Beurre Noisette Powder

Bring the butter to a nut-brown stage in a pan, allow to cool slightly and add the maltose. Season with salt and pepper.

For the Coriander Oil

Blend the coriander and oil, heat in a saucepan until the temperature reaches 60°C, and then chill. When cold, hang in a cheesecloth resting inside a

conical strainer and allow to drain naturally.

For the Amaretto and Duck Jus

Wash all the vegetables thoroughly and cut into chunks, then roast in a large, heavy-bottomed pan until dark. Add tomato purée, roast for a further 2 minutes and deglaze with the white wine.

Add the roasted bones, peppercorns, bay leaves and water and bring to the boil. Simmer for 4 hours and strain.

Reduce liquid until it reaches the desired consistency; it should coat the back of a spoon.

Finish with a dash of amaretto.

To Serve

Roast the duck leg, breast and braised fennel in a frying pan until hot. Next warm up the poached peach in a small pan in the same liquid it was cooked in. Carve the duck breast and leg as desired and arrange on the plate with the fennel and poached peach.

Dress the rest of the plate with 2 teaspoons of the peach and grapefruit gel, one teaspoon of coriander oil and a teaspoon of the noisette powder. Finish with amaretto and duck jus, and Amaretti biscuits

Dessert from 14 North

75% dark chocolate ganache

aquafaba meringue, strawberry compote, strawberry sorbet, strawberry tuile,
basil gel, honeycomb and baby mint

serves 4–6

At the restaurant we always want to ensure that we can accommodate dietary requirements. A great way to do this is by creating 'free from' dishes that appeal to many diners.

This vegan chocolate dessert is a great example, consisting of not only dairy-free ganache, but also meringues using aquafaba. Aquafaba is the water produced from cooking chickpeas and contains many of the same properties found in egg whites. *(continued on page 36)*

75% dark chocolate ganache

Ingredients

Chocolate Ganache

160g distilled water
200g 75% dark chocolate, broken into 2cm pieces

Aquafaba Meringue

1 tin of chickpeas
50g caster sugar

Strawberry Compote

500g fresh ripe strawberries
150g caster sugar

Strawberry Sorbet

1kg strawberry purée (we use 2kg strawberries blended, reduced by half and strained)
300g stock syrup (made with 600g caster sugar, 500ml water, 125g glucose and reduced)
100ml fresh lime juice

Strawberry Tuile

100g strawberry purée (reserved from the Strawberry Sorbet recipe)

Basil Gel

2 ltr filtered water
1 tsp bicarbonate of soda
150g fresh basil
large bowl of ice water
1 lemon
sea salt

Honeycomb

325g caster sugar
50ml distilled water
125g glucose
50g golden syrup
10g bicarbonate of soda
1 tsp vanilla essence

To Serve

baby mint

Method

For the Chocolate Ganache

Bring the water to a boil then remove from the heat. Next add the hot water to a mixing bowl and add the chocolate, mixing until the temperature drops to 38°C.

While warm, pour the mix into non-stick silicone moulds: we prefer an egg shape for our dessert, however, lining small ramekins with cling film would also work.

Allow the mix to cool and set in the fridge for a minimum of 12 hours. Use within 3 days.

Chef's note: *Using 75% chocolate is very important, as more milk in the chocolate will allow the ganache to melt at room temperature.*

For the Aquafaba Meringue

Preheat oven to 60°C/gas ¼

Drain the chickpeas and retain the water (save your chickpeas to use in a salad or to make a garlicky hummus!). Whip the chickpea water and sugar in a food mixer until the mixture reaches soft peaks.

Spread the meringue on a baking paper-lined tray and dry in the oven at 60°C for 4–5 hours.

Store in an airtight container for no longer than 2 days.

For the Strawberry Compote

Cover the strawberries with the sugar and allow to macerate for 12 hours at room temperature. This will release the fructose in the strawberries, giving the compote more body and maintaining the fresh flavours.

Place the mixture into a heavy-bottomed saucepan and cook on a high heat until it reaches a gentle simmer. Allow to cool.

For the Strawberry Sorbet

Set aside 100g of the strawberry purée to use for the strawberry tuile later.

Ensure the ingredients are cold and combine the remaining 900g of strawberry purée, stock syrup and lime juice together, and churn in an ice cream machine until frozen.

Alternatively you could make a strawberry granita by continuously agitating with a fork while freezing.

For the Strawberry Tuile

Thinly spread the purée onto a silicone mat or greaseproof paper-lined tray with a palette knife and dehydrate at 50°C for 4 hours or until crisp.

Store in an airtight container for a maximum of 2 days.

For the Basil Gel

Bring a large pan of water and the bicarbonate of soda to a boil, blanching the basil leaves for 5–10 seconds before refreshing in the ice bath.

Blend the basil in a food processor for a maximum of 30 seconds until smooth and then pass through a fine chinois. Season with a squeeze of lemon and a pinch of sea salt. The bicarbonate of soda will help retain the fresh, green colour of the basil but it will brown quickly. Store in the fridge and use on the same day.

For the Honeycomb

Place the caster sugar, water, glucose and golden syrup in a pan and heat to 152°C using a sugar thermometer. Add the bicarbonate of soda and vanilla essence. While hot, pour carefully onto a large worktop and prick with fork to allow faster cooling.

Once completely cool break into pieces and store in an airtight container.

To Serve

Unmould the chocolate ganache and position in the centre of the plate. Dress the plate with strawberry compote and basil gel. Make a rocher (one-handed quenelle) of the strawberry sorbet and sit this next to the chocolate ganache.

Garnish the dish with the aquafaba meringues, honeycomb and baby mint. Carefully lean the strawberry tuile against the other ingredients to give the dish some height.

Little Fish Cafe

31 North Quay, Douglas IM1 4LB
01624 622518
www.littlefishcafe.com

Shore Rd, Port Erin, Isle of Man IM9 6HL
01624 832084
www.littlefishatthebay.com

Little Fish Cafe opened in April 2014, providing Douglas with a new, vibrant dining option serving fresh fish and fabulous drinks in a friendly atmosphere.

Combining freshly caught local seafood, refreshing cocktails and freshly brewed coffee, Little Fish Café offers all-day dining with stunning quayside views only a short walk from Douglas town centre.

We aim to evoke childhood memories of trips to the seaside, while providing our customers with quality food and service befitting of a more sophisticated dining experience.

Great food brings people together, and our team, with their genuine passion for creating mouth-watering dishes, have created a menu that offers something for everyone – whether an intimate candlelit dinner and cocktails, a quick coffee on the go, or lunch in the sun with a group of friends.

On Saturdays, we serve a well-established brunch menu from 10am to 3pm.

We work with the freshest possible produce and use simple cooking methods to ensure that every dish is showcased to its full potential. Meaning that the food served at Little Fish Cafe is humble, yet delicious.

But we're not just passionate about our food – our drinks menu aims to please, with cold-pressed coffee, iced vanilla lattes and our Bloody Marys taking centre stage.

To complement the food, we also offer carefully selected wines and a dedicated cocktail menu. This allows customers to enjoy the perfect aperitif, a naughty sweet cocktail or simply a refreshing drink in the sunshine.

Starter from Little Fish Cafe

Monkfish fritters
with tomato and chilli jam

serves 4

Ingredients

Tomato and Chilli Jam

500g tomatoes (cored and quartered)
250g granulated sugar
1 red pepper (diced)
3 red chillies (chopped)
1 tsp sea salt
1 tbsp fish sauce
2 tbsp cider vinegar
juice of half a lemon

Monkfish Fritters

140g plain flour (plus extra for dusting)
95g cornflour
375ml Bushy's beer
½ tsp garlic purée
2 monkfish tails
oil for frying
salt to season

Method

For the Tomato and Chilli Jam

Start by making the tomato and chilli jam. This can be made in advance and will last for several months in the fridge.

Add all ingredients to a heavy-bottomed saucepan. Bring to the boil and simmer with no colour for 2 hours. Stir occasionally ensuring that the mixture doesn't stick to the bottom of the pan. Once the mixture is a thick syrup allow to cool. Blitz until smooth and store in an airtight container until required.

For the Monkfish Fritters

A couple of hours before serving, make the batter. Mix together the flours, Bushy's beer and garlic purée with a hand blender until smooth. Pass the batter through a sieve and rest in the fridge until needed.

Preheat a deep-fat fryer to 180°C. Portion the monkfish into 40g pieces, then dust the monkfish in flour. Refresh the batter by running a whisk through it and coat the monkfish in the batter. Shake off the excess and carefully place in the fryer, avoiding any splash back. Deep fry for 2– 3 minutes or until golden and crisp. You may need to fry the monkfish in batches so as not to overcrowd your fryer.

Remove from the fryer and place on some kitchen towel to absorb excess oil. Season with salt immediately.

To Serve

Arrange the monkfish fritters on your plates with the tomato and chilli jam on the side.

Main course from Little Fish Cafe

Penang seafood curry

serves 4

Try to build a good relationship with your fishmonger and always use the freshest and most sustainably sourced seafood available. Feel free to substitute the seafood here for the fish and shellfish of your choice.

Ingredients

Panang Curry Paste

40g large dried chillies (soaked until soft and seeds removed)
1 tsp cumin seeds
1 tsp coriander seeds
1 tbsp roasted peanuts
2 tsp lemongrass (cut into thin rounds)
2 tsp galangal (cut into matchsticks, substitute with ginger if you can't find galangal)
1 tbsp coriander stems
2 tbsp shallots
2 tbsp garlic
1 tsp shrimp paste
1 tsp salt

Seafood Curry

24 queen scallops
200g salmon (cut into 2cm cubes)
200g callig (pollock) (cut into 2cm cubes)

Seafood Curry *(cont)*

1 shallot (small dice)
1 tbsp neutral oil
1 heaped tsp panang curry paste
1 can coconut milk
3 lime leaves (shredded)
1 tsp palm sugar
½ tsp fish sauce
1 tsp smooth peanut butter

Jasmine Rice

325g jasmine rice
575ml water
1 tbsp butter
pinch of salt

To Serve

1 tbsp fresh coriander

(continued on page 44)

Penang seafood curry

Method

For the Panang Curry Paste

Start by making the curry paste. Soak the chillies in water until soft, about half an hour, then remove their seeds. Toast the cumin, coriander seeds and peanuts separately (as they toast at different speeds) in a pan over a medium heat. Roast each until fragrant, about 3–5 minutes. Grind all the seeds together until powdered with a pestle and mortar. Set this aside.

Add the chillies to the mortar and pound until a paste – be patient!

Once a paste consistency has been reached, add the lemongrass, galangal and coriander stems and, again, smash until a paste is formed. Add the peanuts, shallots, garlic and the powdered cumin and coriander seeds. Add the shrimp paste, pound to mix well season with the salt and set aside.

You will require 1 heaped teaspoon to make your curry, the reminder can be frozen down in an ice tray and stored in a freezer bag to be used in the future.

For the Seafood Curry

You are now ready to make the curry. In a heavy-bottomed saucepan cook the shallots in the oil over a low heat, making sure to soften them without colouring them. Add the Panang Paste and fry briefly to allow the flavours to be released – ensuring you don't burn the paste at this stage. Add the coconut milk and bring to the boil. Add the lime leaves, palm sugar and fish sauce, stirring until the sugar has dissolved. Add the peanut butter and simmer for a further 5 minutes.

At this point you can either allow the sauce to cool, store and use the following day or you can finish making the curry.

For the Jasmine Rice

Half an hour before serving the curry, cook the jasmine rice. Put all the ingredients into a saucepan and bring to the boil and simmer. Cook for 16–18 minutes or until all the water has been absorbed.

To Finish the Curry

Bring the sauce back to the boil, bring down to a simmer and poach the seafood in the curry sauce until just cooked – around 5 minutes. Do not stir too much to avoid breaking up the fish.

To Serve

Divide the rice between your plates and ladle the seafood curry alongside ensuring to give each person equal quantities of the seafood. Garnish with fresh coriander.

DAILY
SPECIALS

SARDINE, LOCAL TOMATO + HERB
PANZANELLA   £8

QUEENIE —— , GUACAMOLE,
CHIPOTLE —— HOUSE CHIPS
                            £16

—— FILLET, COURGETTE,
TOMATO + BROWN
BUTTER   £18

—— SEABREAM, CAPER +
—— BUTTER   £19

SATURDAYS
WE SERVE
BRUNCH
10am-3pm

WIFI
password
⇩
"fizzandchips"

COCKTAIL
SPECIAL

PROPOSAL ON THE QUAYSIDE

RASPBERRY, VANILLA, APPLE, RHUBARB,
VODKA, LEMON
                £8.95

Dessert from Little Fish Cafe

Flourless orange and almond cake

serves 4

Cake shouldn't be 'off the menu' because you have a gluten-free diet. Polenta, chestnut flour and, in this case, ground almonds each impart their own unique and deliciously tempting characteristics.

Ingredients

Orange Crème Fraiche

150ml crème fraiche
zest of 1 orange

Flourless Orange and Almond Cake

2 oranges, including the already zested orange
(chopped and pips removed)
7 eggs (separated)

Flourless Orange and Almond Cake *(cont)*

300g caster sugar
325g ground almonds
50g flaked almonds
water

Method

For the Orange Crème Fraiche

Mix the orange zest into the crème fraiche and keep in the fridge until needed.

For the Flourless Orange and Almond Cake

Preheat oven to 200°C /180°C fan oven/gas 6
Add the oranges to a heavy-bottomed pan with just enough water to cover and stew until soft, without colouring. Blend in a food processor and set aside.

In a food mixer (or with an electric whisk) whisk the egg whites, slowly adding half the sugar until you reach soft peaks and set aside in another bowl.

Again using your food mixer whisk the egg yolks with the remaining sugar. Mix in the ground almonds and the stewed oranges, then carefully fold in the egg whites.

Pour the mixture into a 10" lined cake tin. Sprinkle the flaked almonds on top of the cake bake at 180°C in a fan oven for 45-60 minutes (dependent on the depth and width of you cake) or until browned on top and cooked through. Test by inserting a knife into the centre, it should come out clean.

Once cooked, allow to cool on a cake rack and slice into 12 equal portions. Ideally serve while still warm.

To Serve

Place the cake onto a plate and garnish with the orange crème fraiche. Leftovers can be stored in an airtight container and will keep for 3-5 days.

The Courthouse

Athol Street, Douglas, IM1 1LD
01624 672555
www.the-courthouse.com

With its glorious Grade II-listed frontage taking pride of place at the heart of the Douglas financial district, since it opened as a hospitality venue a decade ago The Courthouse has always set the standard for food, fun and entertainment on the Isle of Man.

We are proud to have been awarded the Isle of Man Tourism's 'Taste Isle of Man' award for the highest quality-assured food and service for the last 10 years. Our business has also been featured in many national newspapers and we were also chosen as the venue of the month in both the *BBC Good Food magazine* and *Olive*.

Our kitchen has undergone an exciting transformation in recent times, with the arrival of our creative sous-chef, Darren Taylor, who has designed the recipes featured here. Darren is supremely innovative and has already put his stamp on our current, wide-ranging food options. He is now busy working on an exciting new menu, which promises to be our best yet.

As well as retaining popular Manx dishes, with superb local meat and fish still to the fore, the emphasis will be on providing a more varied choice of food, with the introduction of Mediterranean cuisine.

One tradition that The Courthouse restaurant is proud to retain is the exclusive relationship it enjoys with Corney and Barrow, one of the world's most respected wine merchants. The company has a royal warrant dating back to 1912, ensuring that The Courthouse will continue to serve the finest wines on the Island.

The establishment has always catered to a broad market: the business clientele who populate the dining room at lunchtime; to those who want a place to chill and relax over drinks and cocktails in the magnificent main bar area; and then there's the younger set who have made the Courthouse Nightclub the trendiest late-night location on the Island, attracting some of the biggest DJs in the business.

As General Manager, Stewart Dillon explained: 'The unique advantage of The Courthouse is that it is the one venue on the Island that can offer such a comprehensive choice of entertainment, all under one roof. The work we have undertaken in recent months is now behind us and we are delighted with how it all looks. The entire venue is now looking better than ever, there's nowhere quite like it on the Isle of Man.'

Everything's well and truly back on song at The Courthouse, you could say!

Starter from The Courthouse

Seven Kingdom Douglas dry gin-cured salmon with cucumber and wasabi

serves 6

Ingredients

1 side of fresh salmon

The Cure

50g sugar
50g table salt
25g lemon zest (microplaned)
100ml Douglas dry gin
10 white peppercorns (whole)
25g fresh Manx dill (chopped)

Wasabi Mayo

2 tubes wasabi paste
1 jar mayonnaise

Cucumber Jelly

2 fresh cucumbers
1 tbsp white wine vinegar
4–5 sheets gelatine

Cucumber Pickle

100ml water
40ml white wine vinegar
10ml olive oil
10g shallot (finely sliced)
1 garlic clove (sliced)
1 sprig fresh thyme
2g salt
2 fresh cucumbers

Torched Cucumber

2 cucumber seed sections (reserved from the cucumber pickle)
2 tbsp olive oil
a pinch of salt and pepper

Method

Begin by preparing the salmon. Combine the sugar, salt, lemon, gin, pepper and dill in a bowl and place the salmon on a tray. Coat both sides of the salmon in the marinade, ensuring the mixture is evenly distributed. Cover with cling film and leave in the fridge overnight.

For the Wasabi Mayo

Mix the wasabi with the mayonnaise and set aside for later.

For the Cucumber Jelly

Roughly chop the cucumber, place in a blender and blitz. Pass through a sieve, then add the 1 tablespoon of vinegar and gently warm. Soak the gelatine in cold water and add to the warm cucumber and vinegar mix. Mix well until dissolved then add to the rest of the cucumber. Mix well again then place in a tray that has been lined with cling film. Put in the fridge to set.

For the Cucumber Pickle

Prepare the pickling liquor for the cucumber – combine the water, vinegar, oil, shallots, garlic, thyme and salt in a pan. Bring to the boil then remove from the heat and set aside for 20 minutes to infuse.

To prepare the cucumber, cut around the seeded part so that it is square and put aside for the torched cucumber. Cut the flesh part into ribbons or shape into ovals and place in the pickle, leave until you're ready to serve.

For the Torched Cucumber Hearts

Season the seeded part that you kept with salt and pepper. Drizzle with olive oil and burn one side with a blow torch just before plating up.

To Serve

Rinse the salmon in cold water and pat dry with kitchen towel. Slice or cut any way you like and you're ready to plate up.

Arrange salmon slices on the top of each plate, add two or three slices of the cucumber jelly then scatter on some torched cucumber heart pieces. Finally add some drops of wasabi mayonnaise and cucumber pickle.

Manx pork fillet

with Manx chorizo, tomato and whitebeans, and herb oil

serves 8

Ingredients

4 Manx pork fillets
1 red onion
1 garlic clove
1 stick Close Leece Farm chorizo
1 pack Manx vine cherry tomatoes
1 tin butterbeans
salt and pepper

Herb Oil

1 bunch parsley
1 punnet basil
½ lemon (zest and juice)
1 bottle extra virgin olive oil
(or Manx rapeseed oil)
salt and pepper

Method

Preheat oven to 180°C/gas 6

Start with the pork fillet by removing the sinew (silver skin). Once removed, set aside.

Finely dice the red onion and garlic, dice the chorizo, cut tomatoes in half and open, drain and wash the butterbeans under cold water. Keep all separate before you start cooking.

For the Herb Oil

Place all herb oil ingredients in a food blender and blitz, then pass through a clean cloth.

For the Pork

Season your pork with salt and pepper and the herb oil, then place in a hot pan to sear on all sides. Next, place on an oven tray and bake for 6–8 minutes. The pork should be slightly pink in the centre when cooked. Allow to rest 6–8 minutes.

While the pork is in the oven, place the chorizo in the same pan you seared the pork in and sweat to allow the natural oils to come out. Add the onion and garlic, and cook until the onions are soft. Then add in the tomatoes and cook for 3 minutes. Finally add the beans and cook for a further 5 minutes.

To Serve

Once the pork has rested, thinly slice each fillet. Place a portion of the chorizo, tomato and whitebeans onto each plate and top with the pork.

Dessert from The Courthouse

Panna cotta

FV elderflower wine, macerated strawberries and basil jelly

serves 8

Ingredients

Panna Cotta

500ml full-fat milk
500ml double cream
150g caster sugar
2 vanilla pods
4 sheets gelatine

Foraging Vintners Elderflower Wine Strawberries

250g fresh strawberries
2–3 tbsp caster sugar
2–3 bottles of Foraging Vintners Elderflower Wine

Fresh Basil Jelly

585ml cold water
500g caster sugar
4 sheets gelatine
3 bunches fresh basil

Method

For the Panna Cotta

Warm the milk, cream and caster sugar, and split the vanilla pods before submerging in the liquid, to allow the seeds to come out into the saucepan into the milk mixture.

While the milk is warming, soak the gelatine in cold water. Once the milk is warm, take the vanilla pods out of the milk. Remove the gelatine from the water and stir it into the milk until dissolved. When it's all dissolved pour the mixture into a jug and allow to cool a little. Be sure to mix well so the vanilla seeds don't all sink to the bottom. Once it's cooled, pour the mixture into the moulds or glasses of your choice.

For the Macerated Strawberries

Take the green stems off the strawberries and place them into a bowl. Coat them with caster sugar, then pour in the elderflower wine and allow to marinate for a few hours.

For the Basil Jelly

Place the water and sugar in a saucepan and bring to the boil while the gelatine soaks in cold water. Once boiling, remove the pan from the heat and add the gelatine to the sugar syrup; stir until the gelatine is dissolved completely. While the syrup is still hot add the fresh basil and blitz until smooth, then pass through a fine sieve and pour into a deep tray lined with heat resistant cling film.

To Serve

Once the panna cotta and basil jelly have set, and the strawberries have had time to marinate, assemble your dish. Place a slice of the basil jelly on each panna cotta, then top with a portion of the macerated strawberries. Garnish with a few basil leaves to taste.

Ocean

North Quay, Douglas, IM1 4LB
01624 622000
www.oceanrestaurant.im

Ocean, which opened in Douglas in November 2017, is a cool, crisp contemporary environment that lends itself to a relaxed dining experience as well as having a friendly family feel. Ocean provides a warm, comfortable setting for any event, whether this be a business lunch, a family celebration or a chance to gather some friends together and enjoy a fabulous brunch on Saturday and Sundays.

To complement the style of our restaurant, Steve, our head chef, and his team have created a modern contemporary British/European menu that focuses on using sustainable and responsibly harvested seafood from our local waters.

Fresh lobster and crab are brought through the door by Alan at Cushlin Seafoods, who catches these from the crystal clear waters in Niarbyl Bay off the west coast of the Island.

The food scene on the Island in recent years has continued to expand and develop, and with this comes numerous dietary requirements for customers, such as coeliac, dairy and seafood intolerances.

Here at Ocean the whole team are passionate in creating an environment where our guests are comfortable and cared for, and within our capable kitchen we make sure guests with such needs can still experience 'Exquisite Coastal Dining'.

At Ocean we have an exclusive wine list to match our exclusive seafood offering, anything from a simple Chilean Sauvignon Blanc to a complex Pauillac from Bordeaux. Our wonderful guests can soak up the picturesque marina views with a variety of after-dinner drinks, whether this be a beautiful Armagnac, a matured port or even a classic Irish Coffee.

Starter from Ocean
Crab and courgette cannelloni
serves 4

Ingredients

Pickled Cucumber

½ cucumber
50g white wine vinegar
50g water
100g caster sugar
2 bay leaves
5 coriander seeds

Avocado Purée

2 avocados
juice of ½ a lemon
Maldon sea salt

Crab Filling

200g Cushlin seafood's white crab meat
(check carefully to ensure all pieces of shell have
been removed)
80g crème fraiche
½ tsp each of finely chopped chives, parsley and
dill
juice of ½ a lemon
Maldon sea salt

Courgettes for Cannelloni

24 x 1mm ribbons of courgette
(sliced on a mandolin)

To Serve

watercress to garnish

Method

For the Pickled Cucumber

Peel the cucumber lengthways into ribbons.
Turn the cucumber over when you reach the
seeds and peel the other side. Set aside.

Put all the other ingredients into a pan and
simmer for 10 minutes.

Remove from the heat and allow to cool.
Remove the bay leaves and coriander seeds.

Add the cucumber ribbons to the liquid and
leave to pickle for 2 hours.

For the Avocado Purée

Blitz the avocado and lemon juice in a food
processor and add salt to taste.

Push through a fine sieve for a smoother purée.
Store in a disposable piping bag until needed.

For the Crab Filling

Mix the crab meat, crème fraiche, herbs and
lemon juice together and add salt to taste. Set
aside for later.

To Assemble

Lay down 3 courgette ribbons, overlapping the
long edges by 2mm. Lightly salt and leave for 2
minutes, the salt allows the courgette to break
down and become more pliable.

Place 1 tablespoon of the crab mix at one of
the short ends of the courgettes and roll to make
cannelloni. Do not roll too tightly or the crab will
come out of the sides.

Repeat the process until you have 8 cannelloni.
Place 2 in the centre of each plate.

Remove the cucumber from the pickle and
place onto kitchen paper to remove any excess
liquid.

Roll each piece of cucumber around a thick
handled wooden spoon or similar to form cylinders
and place at equal spaces around the plate.

Gently squeeze 2 pea-sized dots of avocado
purée between each cylinder of cucumber and 2
on top of each cannelloni roll. Garnish with small
pieces of watercress.

Main course from Ocean

Roast salmon fillet
with romesco sauce and crispy prawns

serves 4

Ingredients

Romesco Sauce

1 large red pepper (roasted)
3 garlic cloves
1 tbsp flaked almonds (toasted)
2 tbsp sherry vinegar
½ tsp smoked paprika
8 tbsp extra virgin olive oil
Maldon sea salt to taste

Crispy Prawns

2 whole eggs
2 tbsp sriracha sauce
8 peeled and deveined king prawns (size 16/20)
80g plain flour
120g panko breadcrumbs
1 tsp Maldon sea salt (mixed through the flour)

4 x 140g salmon portions scored at 1mm spaces
(ask your fishmonger to do this for you)
16 x 5mm slices of steamed new potatoes
12 pieces of tenderstem broccoli
oil for frying
Maldon sea salt to taste

Method

For the Romesco Sauce

Blitz all the ingredients, except the olive oil, in a food processor until roughly chopped. Slowly trickle in the olive oil until all the oil is added.

For the Crispy Prawns

Lightly beat the 2 eggs and sriracha sauce in a bowl. Toss the prawns through the seasoned flour, then coat with the egg before coating with the breadcrumbs. Set aside.

To Cook

Heat a large non-stick frying pan on a medium heat and add a drizzle of oil.

Pat the salmon fillets dry with kitchen paper, lightly season with salt then gently place skin-side down in the pan and turn the heat down to low.

After 2 minutes add the slices of steamed new potato and cook until golden brown. At this point, put the broccoli in a steamer for 2 minutes.

Deep-fry the king prawns for 2–3 minutes until golden brown. Turn the salmon over and remove the pan from the heat.

To Assemble.

On a large bowl or plate, place 1 tablespoon of romesco sauce. Place the salmon fillet just off centre then arrange 3 pieces of broccoli to the left of the salmon and 4 pieces of sautéed potatoes to the right.

Place the king prawns between the broccoli and potatoes.

Dessert from Ocean

Chocolate tart

with raspberry sorbet and almond glass

serves 8

Ingredients for Chocolate Tart Base

155g butter (plus more for greasing the tart tin)
100g icing sugar
200g flour
75g almonds or hazelnuts (finely chopped)
¼ tsp salt
1 ½ tsp orange zest
1 egg (beaten)

Chocolate Tart Filling

365g 70% dark chocolate pistoles
25g honey
390ml Isle of Man Creamery whipping cream
85g butter

Chocolate tart makes 8 portions

Method

For the Chocolate Tart Base

Start by making the tart base. Cream the butter and icing sugar together, and then add the flour, almonds or hazelnuts, salt and zest. Add 30g of the beaten egg and slowly mix together until it forms a dough. Lightly knead to form a ball, wrap in cling film and rest for 1 hour in the fridge before use. Preheat the oven to 170°C/150°C fan oven/gas 3

Remove the pastry dough from the fridge and roll it out onto a flat surface to a thickness of 5mm. Use a 23cm loose-bottomed tart tin and line with greaseproof paper. Next, carefully line the tin with the rolled pastry.

Brush the tart base with the egg wash and blind bake until the tart is golden brown, about 15–20 minutes. Allow to cool while you make the chocolate filling.

For the Chocolate Tart Filling

For the filling, place the chocolate pistoles in a large mixing bowl. In a pan, heat the honey with the cream until hot, being careful not to boil. Once hot, pour over the chocolate pistoles and stir until the chocolate has melted. When the chocolate has melted, add the butter and continue to stir until fully melted.

(continued on page 69)

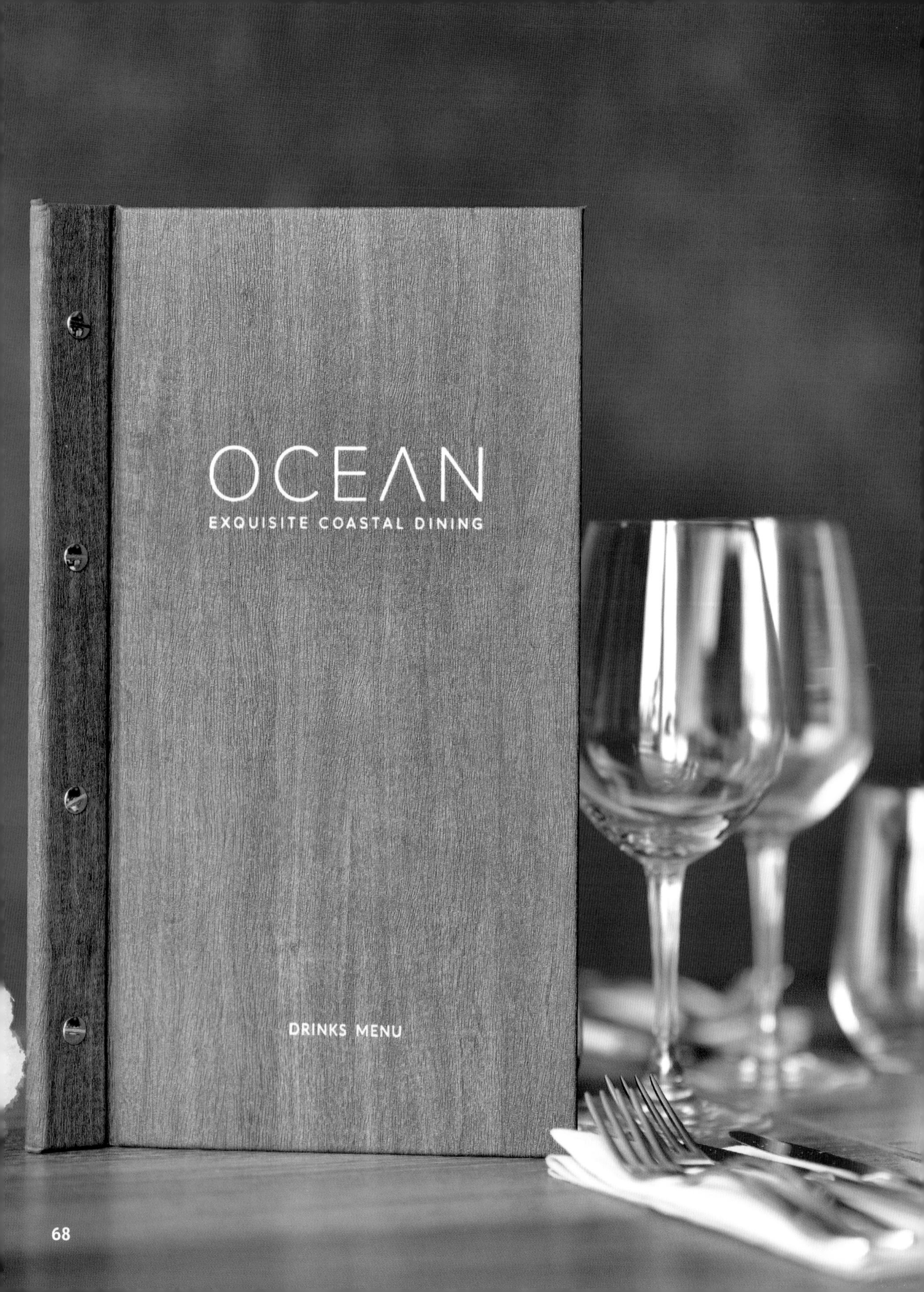
OCEAN
EXQUISITE COASTAL DINING
DRINKS MENU

Chocolate tart

Ingredients for Raspberry Sorbet

750g raspberries
3 tbsp lemon juice
½ tsp good quality vanilla extract

275g caster sugar

Makes 8 portions

Method

Blitz the raspberries, lemon juice and vanilla extract in a food processor, then pass through a sieve to remove the seeds.

Place the caster sugar into a medium-sized pan with 1 tablespoon of cold water and gently heat until it becomes a colourless syrup.

Allow the mixture to cool. Reserve 4 tablespoons of the mixture to garnish the plate, before churning in an ice cream maker according to manufacturer's instructions.

Store in a freezer until needed.

Ingredients for Almond Glass

150g caster sugar
50g flaked almonds

Method

Add the sugar and 1 teaspoon of water to a medium-sized pan and heat gently until a rich brown colour is achieved. Next add the flaked almonds and carefully mix through with a heatproof spoon.

Using 2 sheets of baking parchment, or silicone mats, very carefully pour the caramel as evenly as possible into the middle of 1 sheet, then place the second sheet on top. Using a rolling pin, gently roll the caramel until it is approx 1mm thick. Allow to cool in a dry place.

To Assemble

Take 4 plates and place 1 tablespoon of raspberry sauce in the middle of each plate. Hit gently with the back of a spoon to achieve a splatter effect.

Cut the tart into even-sized portions (as big or as small as you like) and place in the centre of each plate. Scoop out 4 balls of sorbet and place at the top of the tart. Break the now-cooled almond glass into shards and place on the tart.

Tanroagan

9 Ridgeway Street, Douglas, IM1 1EW
01624 612355
www.tanroagan.co.uk

Tanroagan, simply translated as Shell (Tan) Scallop (Roagan) from Manx Gaelic, is a family run restaurant owned by the Mowat family.

The restaurant is located a few feet from North Quay, home to Douglas marina and has gained a deserved reputation as a popular leisure and dining-out destination.

Joan and Graham Mowat took over the reins from local chef and fisherman Butch Buttery in April 2006, despite coming to the Island to retire after a lengthy career in hospitality. The following day the restaurant hosted TV celebrities, the Hairy Bikers, and has gone on to welcome many visiting celebrities over the years, with the Island being a popular destination for film and tv show productions. However, the real stars at Tanroagan are the many visitors and locals who come time and time again to enjoy the fresh and tastiest seafood found on the Island.

Located in the middle of the Irish Sea it is no wonder the Isle of Man boasts some of the very best fish and seafood in the British Isles. Famous locally and around the world for its delicious Manx scallops, queenies and lobsters, the Island has become an established destination for foodies looking for a great culinary experience as well enjoying the fantastic scenery, activities and heritage the Isle of Man has to offer. A massive boost to the culinary experience has been the growth of small independent food and drink producers, allowing restaurants like Tanroagan to offer diners a true taste of the Island through dishes incorporating produce and ingredients sourced here on the Island.

The entrance, with ceiling-to-floor windows, patio doors and a contemporary façade, welcomes you when arriving at Tanroagan. The time-worn and creaky wooden floor boards have been replaced by a beautiful Spanish tiled floor with built-in underfloor heating, essential throughout the Manx wintery months. Featured lighting, driftwood tables and candlelit tables combine to create a vibrant and exciting dining experience.

There is simply no better place to experience Manx-sourced cuisine and the delights of the sea than at Tanroagan, the Island's long-established specialist seafood restaurant, where fresh seafood really is the dish of the day.

Starter from Tanroagan

Crab toasties

serves approx 6 portions

Ingredients

50g white crab meat
50g brown crab meat
100g mayonnaise
50g fresh breadcrumbs
100g cream cheese

1 tsp soy sauce (dark)
ciabatta or sourdough bread
(cut into slices 1cm thick and lightly toasted)
lemon
parsley

Method

Mix all the ingredients in a bowl, except the ciabatta, until incorporated. Refrigerate the mixture until required.

To Serve

Preheat oven to 200°C/180°C fan oven/gas 6

Put 2 slices of ciabatta per person on an oven tray, place a tablespoon of the crab mix on each slice.
Bake in the preheated oven for 4 minutes. Place on a plate and garnish with lemon and parsley.

TANROAGAN - STARTER

Main course from Tanroagan

Seabass involtini from the Italian for little bundle, a traditional Italian dish

serves 6

Ingredients

Seabass

240g mozzarella cheese (grated)
180g raisins
60g pine nuts (toasted)
fresh parsley (chopped)
12 seabass fillets (skinned and boneless)
breadcrumbs
salt and pepper

Pea Purée

500g frozen peas
salt
¼ tsp lemon juice

Potatoes

baby new potatoes (4–5 per person)
butter
olive oil
thyme (freshly chopped)
salt and pepper

To Serve

pea shoots
pesto
lemon

Method

For the Seabass

In a bowl mix the cheese, raisins, pine nuts and parsley together.

On a board, lightly flatten the seabass fillets with a rolling pin and season, then top each fillet with the cheese mix. Starting from the tail, roll up each fillet in cling film to create a sausage shape and refrigerate until required. Reserve the breadcrumbs for later.

For the Pea Purée

Cook the peas in salted water for 3 minutes. Put the peas in a blender with the lemon juice and a little of the cooking water then blitz the peas, adding more water if required to create a thick, smooth purée. Taste and season

For the Potatoes

Allow 4–5 baby new potatoes per person. Boil in their skins until cooked. Drain and scrape the skins off. Place in bowl with seasoning, olive oil, butter and fresh chopped thyme.

To Cook and Assemble

Preheat oven to 200°C/180°C fan oven/gas 6

Before cooking remove the seabass fillets from the cling film and roll in the breadcrumbs. Place on baking paper on a baking tray and drizzle with a little olive oil. Cook for 6 minutes, cut in half through the middle and put back in the oven for 2 minutes.

Seabass fillets can vary in size so check they are cooked through before serving. Leave in the oven to cook a little while longer if needed.

Place the pea purée in the centre of a plate and arrange circles of seabass on and around the pea purée.

Place the potatoes between the seabass rolls, garnish with pea shoots, pesto and lemon.

Limoncello cheesecake with ice cream
serves 6-8

Ingredients

Shortbread Base

100g butter (softened)
50g caster sugar, plus extra to sprinkle
160g plain flour

Cheesecake Mix

3 sheets of gelatine
400ml double cream
200ml milk
290g caster sugar

2 lemons (zest and juice)
300g cream cheese

Limoncello Glaze

200g caster sugar
200ml limoncello
4 gelatine leaves

To Serve

your favourite ice cream
whipped cream
lemon curd

Method

For the Shortbread Base

Put the butter into a mixing bowl and beat with a wooden spoon, or by electric mixer, until soft. Add the sugar and mix well until fully incorporated. Sift the flour into the mixture and stir to a firm, smooth paste.

Line a 20cm/8 inch springform tin with a parchment circle, press the shortbread mixture into the ring and smooth into a neat circle, using the back of a cutlery spoon.

Prick evenly with a fork, well into the dough, and chill until firm.

Preheat oven to 190°C/170°C fan oven/gas 5

Cook the shortbread on the middle shelf of the oven for 20–25 minutes, or until a pale biscuit colour with no grey patches in the middle. Remove from the oven and leave to cool.

For the Cheesecake Mix

Put the gelatine into cold water to soak for 5 minutes. Heat the cream and milk together in a saucepan with the sugar, lemon juice and finely grated zest until the sugar is dissolved. Remove the gelatine from the water and put in the hot liquid. Leave to cool slightly (do not let it go cold) and mix in the cream cheese.

Pour over the shortbread base and leave to set, then refrigerate.

For the Limoncello Glaze

Put the sugar and limoncello in a saucepan and bring to the boil until the sugar is dissolved.

Put the gelatine into cold water to soak for 5 minutes, then take it out of the water and add to the hot liquid. Leave to cool.

When the cheesecake has set and chilled, top with the cool glaze, refrigerate and leave to set.

To Serve

Remove the cheesecake carefully from the tin and cut into wedges with a knife dipped in hot water.

Serve with your favourite ice cream or whipped cream, topped with lemon curd.

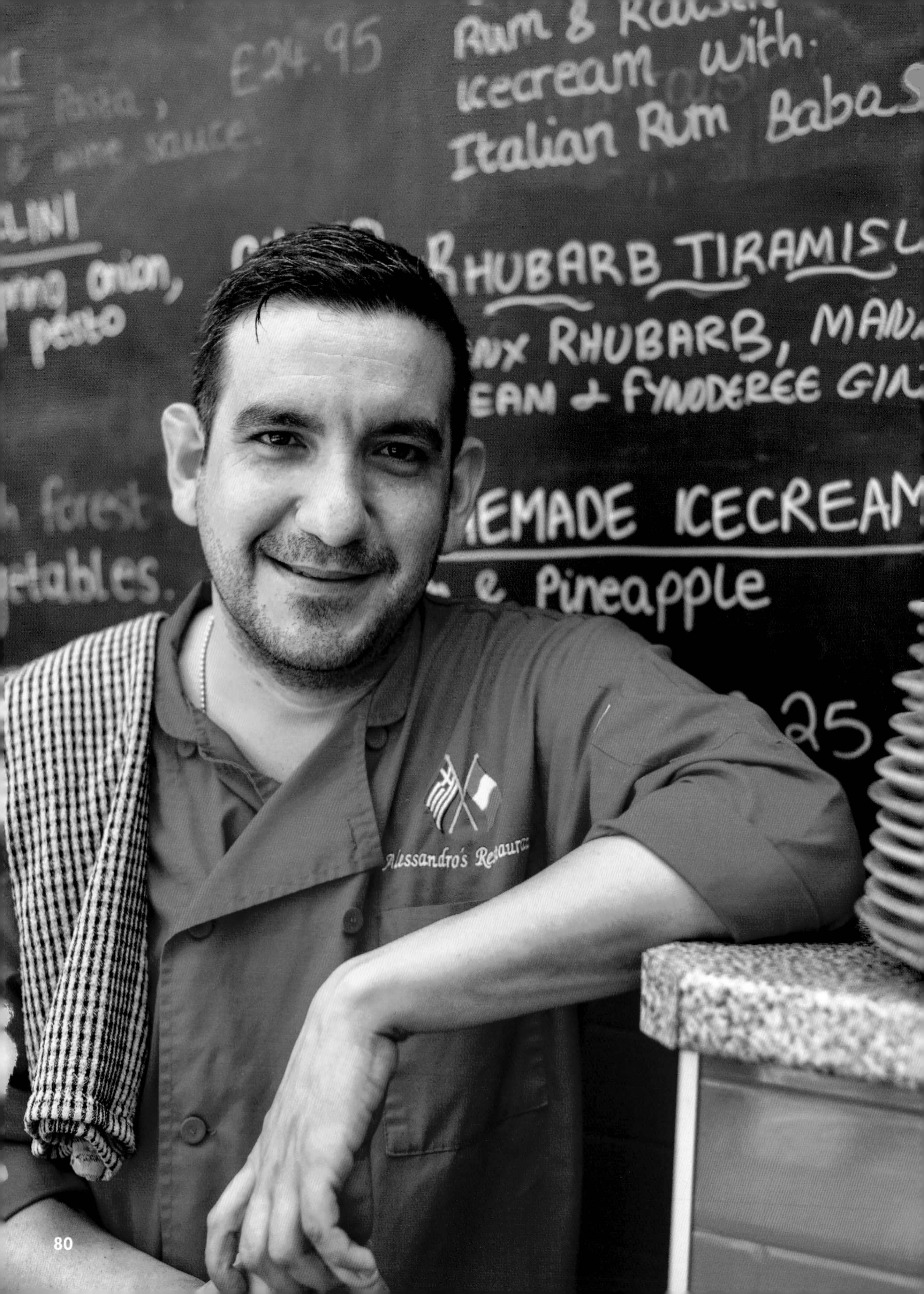

£24.95
Icecream with
Italian Rum
pesto
RHUBARB
Pineapple

Alessandro's

13–15 Castle Street, Douglas, IM1 2EX
01624 626003
www.alessandrosiom.co.uk

Influenced by Italian trattorias, Greek tavernas and French bistros, Alessandro's is a truly Mediterranean restaurant, ideally located in the heart of Douglas in the Isle of Man, on the first floor of the old Victoria Arcade with a quaint but informal atmosphere, unique food and drink choices, simplicity and quality.

Our menu embraces the Mediterranean way of life and is a diverse collection of cross-cultural influences spanning the Mediterranean, with delicate flavours predominating. We emphasise amazing olive oils, artisan cheese, grains and fresh local fish, meat and vegetables.

With respect for the local and imported ingredients and our 'cooked to order' philosophy, our Sicilian head chef, German Sottile, and his team produce a seasonal cuisine that is a mixture of traditional family dishes and contemporary and imaginative variations.

The sensibility in knowing what to do with good ingredients is our strong point, such as the ability to deliciously vary the final taste with a change in the basic recipes. In a sense, like eating at a friend's house.

We have a tremendous respect for the gifts of nature and treat food with love and simplicity. We love food, love cooking and we do everything with passion.

We offer a wide choice of reliable, popular British, Manx and Mediterranean cuisine with local game and seafood specialities on the menu when in season, signature dishes and innovative homemade desserts.

We have an interesting wine list with over 50 different wines, over 25 artisan gins and a large cocktail, beer and spirit menu.

Whatever the occasion, from recharging your batteries after shopping, a business lunch, a party or just going out with friends, family or colleagues, our long-serving restaurant manager Daniele Saporito and his team will welcome you at Alessandro's and will make your visit a memorable one.

Starter from Alessandro's
Goat's cheese bon bons
serves 2

Ingredients

230g Close Leece Farm Manx goat's cheese
100g sun blushed tomatoes in oil
50g black olives (stoned)
1 sprig Staarvey Farm rosemary
2 free-range eggs
250ml milk
250g flour
250g breadcrumbs (from sourdough or focaccia)
100g Close Leese Farm Manx chorizo
Manx Ellerslie virgin rapeseed oil for frying

To Serve

cooked peas and edamame beans
Manx honey
Staarvey Farm edible flowers and micro herbs

Method

Empty the goat's cheese into a large bowl and leave to come to room temperature. Drain the tomatoes and roughly chop, then chop the olives and the rosemary. Add everything to the goat's cheese, mix well and roll into golf-ball sized bon bons.

Next crack the eggs into a bowl, add the milk and whisk together to create an eggwash.

Place the flour onto a tray and spread out the breadcrumbs on a separate tray. Roll the goat's cheese bon bons through the flour, then into the eggwash, then into the breadcrumbs and roll around until completely covered in crumbs.

Place in the fridge to firm up.

Cut the chorizo into cubes or thin slices and fry until crispy. Keep warm.

Put enough oil in a heavy-bottomed pan or deep-fat fryer and fry the bon bons in batches until they are golden brown (this should take 1–2 minutes). Take them out with a slotted spoon and place on paper kitchen towel to remove any excess oil.

Put peas and edamame beans in the centre of a plate and place the bon bons on top. Drizzle on some Manx honey and decorate with micro herbs and a few edible flowers.

Main course from Alessandro's
Thyme for fish
serves 2

Ingredients

4 slices of Deverau's smoked bacon
½kg potatoes

Sauce

2 banana shallots (peeled and very finely chopped)
75ml dry white wine
75ml water
75ml double cream
a few springs of Staarvey Farm thyme
250g butter (diced)

Chard

½ kg Staarvey Farm rainbow chard or spinach
2 garlic cloves (sliced)
freshly squeezed lemon juice, to taste

2 whiting fillets, about 150g each, skin on
(you can use hake, cod or haddock fillets)
Manx Ellerslie virgin rapeseed oil for roasting
and frying
lemon wedges
salt and freshly ground pepper

Method

For the Bacon

Grill the bacon until crispy and keep warm.

For the Potato Wedges

Preheat oven 200°C/gas 6
Put a large pan of salted water on to boil. Scrub the potatoes clean, then cut the potatoes into chunky wedges. Add to the pan of boiling water and parboil for 8 minutes. Drain in a colander and leave to steam dry for a couple of minutes.

Transfer to a roasting tray and add a few tablespoons of rapeseed oil, salt and pepper. Toss together so all the wedges are coated in the oil, then spread out in one layer. Cook in the hot oven for 30 minutes until golden, crisp and cooked through.

For the Sauce

Place the shallots, white wine and water into a heavy-based pan and bring to the boil. Let them simmer until reduced to a quarter, then add the cream and boil for one minute. Reduce the heat and add the thyme and 125g butter. Whisk vigorously until you have a lovely silky sauce – do not let the sauce boil or it will separate. Remove from the heat, season and keep warm.

For the Chard

Wash the chard. Melt the rest of the butter in a frying pan over a medium heat, then add the garlic and fry for 30 seconds. Add the wet chard and a little lemon juice to the pan and cook for 4–5 minutes until tender. Keep warm.

For the Fish

Season the whiting (or whatever fish you use) with salt and pepper. Heat a frying pan over a medium heat and add 2–3 tablespoons of

To Serve

rapeseed oil. Add the fillets skin side down and cook for 3–4 minutes. The skin should be crisp. Turn and cook the other side for 2–3 minutes.

Place the fish on serving plates, lay the crispy bacon on top and spoon the sauce around the fish. Serve with the potato wedges, wilted chard and lemon wedges.

Dessert from Alessandro's
Summer tiramisu
serves 4

Ingredients

Stewed Rhubarb

500g fresh rhubarb
50g caster sugar
½ tsp fresh ginger (shredded)
30ml water
dash of grenadine for colour
30g butter
25ml Manx Fynoderee Gin

Cream Filling

3 egg yolks
85g caster sugar
1 vanilla pod
250g mascarpone cheese
150ml double cream

To Serve

Savoiardi biscuits
fresh mint

Method

For the Rhubarb

Wash and trim the rhubarb. If the stalks are thick, remove the outer layer. Cut into 1–2cm pieces. Add to a saucepan with the sugar, ginger, water, grenadine and butter and bring to the boil, then reduce the heat and simmer until the rhubarb is soft. Drain the rhubarb and reserve the liquid. Let cool.

Put the cooled rhubarb liquid in a bowl and add the Fynoderee Gin.

For the Cream Filling

Place a metal whisking bowl over a pan of just simmering water. Add the egg yolks and caster sugar to the bowl and whisk until they become thick and foamy. The mixture will become pale and roughly double in volume. Take care not to overheat the mixture or it will turn to scrambled egg. The mixture should be quite thick. Set aside to cool, but don't refrigerate.

In a separate bowl, add the vanilla seeds to the mascarpone and gently mix and soften using the back of a fork. In a third bowl, gently whisk the double cream.

Fold the egg mixture into the mascarpone and mix thoroughly. Finally, very gently fold in the double cream to the mix.

To Assemble

To assemble the tiramisu, dip Savoiardi biscuits into the cooled liquid (reserving some of the liquid for a garnish) and place a layer into the bottom of individual serving glasses or bowls. Then add a layer of the mascarpone and cream mix, followed by rhubarb and biscuits and continue until your glass or bowl is full.

Cover and place in the fridge for 2 hours to set.

Decorate with fresh mint and a few drops of the rhubarb and gin liquid.

Enzo's

52 Bucks Rd, Douglas, IM1 3AD
01624 622653
www.facebook.com/Enzos-Restaurant-447954141951669

It has been over six years now that Enzo's Restaurant has operated in the heart of Douglas in Bucks Road. Our extensive menu showcases an excellent variety of dishes made using local produce and the freshest ingredients; the creation of a cuisine that has brought alive those locally sourced ingredients in well presented and flavoured dishes, appreciated by our local and visiting customers.

Head Chef at Enzo's, Stuart Fenney, qualified at St Helens College catering school, and gained a diploma in Professional Cookery. He moved to the Isle of Man in 2006 and, after experience in the hotel industry, worked in various restaurants eventually taking the post of Head Chef at Enzo's in 2013.

At Enzo's, in the heart of Douglas, you will find a restaurant able to cater for any occasion with the upmost professional manner. A standard of food and service that the Isle of Man can be proud of. We are here to deliver, day after day, a dining experience under the meticulous supervision of Enzo and the professional commitment of our team.

Starter from Enzo's

Twice baked Manx vintage Cheddar cheese soufflé

caramelised onions, Staarvey Farm organic leaves and balsamic glaze

serves approx 10 portions

Ingredients

Soufflé

100g butter
120g Laxey Mill plain flour (sieved)
250ml full-fat milk
250ml double cream (plus extra for baking)
500g Manx vintage Cheddar (grated plus extra for baking)
6 egg yolks (beaten)
5 egg whites (whipped)
1 tsp English mustard
salt and pepper to taste
10 ramekins buttered and dusted with grated cheese

Glazed Onions

2 tbsp olive oil
3 large red onions (thinly sliced)
2 tbsp brown sugar
2 tbsp balsamic vinegar
salt

To Serve

Staarvey Farm organic leaves
balsamic glaze

Method

For the Soufflé

Preheat oven to 150°C/gas 2

Gently melt the butter in a saucepan, add the sieved flour and stir to make a roux blond and gradually add the milk and cream.

Next add the grated cheese into the mixture over a low heat and put the pan aside to cool down slightly.

Add the beaten egg yolks and fold in the whipped egg whites. Season the mixture with salt and pepper and stir in the English mustard, then pour the mixture into the ramekins and bake in a bain-marie in the preheated oven for about 25 minutes.

Rest once cooked until cooled down, before you take out of the ramekins.

For the Glazed Onions

Heat the oil in a large frying pan. Add the sliced red onions and add a pinch of salt to taste. Stir the onions occasionally to make sure that they don't burn and cook on low to medium heat.

When the onions are softened, add the brown sugar and the balsamic vinegar, this will start to caramelise. Stir until the onions are fully cooked.

Take the onions out of the pan and cool down in a tray over greaseproof paper.

To Double Bake the Soufflé

Preheat oven to 180°C/gas 4

Turn the soufflés the correct way up and place in a small baking dish over a sheet of greaseproof paper.

Pour a generous amount of Manx double cream and sprinkle this with grated cheese.

Bake in the preheated oven for 10–15 minutes.

To Serve

Serve the soufflés over Staarvey Farm organic leaves with caramelised onions and drizzled balsamic glaze.

Main course from Enzo's
Rack of Manx lamb
dauphinoise potatoes and port wine jus
serves 2

Ingredients

Dauphinoise Potatoes

potatoes (peeled, enough to fill your dish)
500ml double cream
500ml full-fat milk
Manx Cheddar cheese (grated)

Sauce

½ shallot (chopped)
20ml Port wine

80ml homemade beef bone stock
1 x 4-bone rack of Manx lamb (French trimmed)
oil for frying

Method

For the Dauphinoise Potatoes

Preheat oven to 180°C/gas 4
Slice the potatoes with a mandolin. Place the potatoes in layers and cover those with a mixture of the cream and milk. Sprinkle the grated cheese on top.
Bake for approx. 30 minutes.

For the Sauce

Gently fry the chopped shallots until translucent, add the port wine and reduce, then add the beef stock.
Reduce this and simmer.

To Serve

Preheat oven to 200°C/gas 6

Season the rack of lamb.
Heat the oil in a frying pan and sear the lamb on the fat side until coloured, then place the meat on a baking tray and cook in the preheated oven for about 12–15 minutes.
Once the meat is cooked pink, rest for 2 minutes.
Assemble the dauphinoise potatoes on the plate, preferably shaped with a 2-inch cutter.
Carve the rack of lamb and place this next to the potatoes,
Gently pour the port wine sauce onto the plate and serve immediately.

Dessert from Enzo's

Chocolate and orange cheesecake

with cookies ice cream

serves 10

Ingredients

Cheesecake

half a pack of digestive biscuits
150g butter
250g cream cheese
100g caster sugar
200ml double cream
300g dark cooking chocolate
1 whole orange (squeezed and the peel grated)
1 leaf of gelatine

Cookies Ice Cream

700ml double cream
300ml full-fat milk
1 vanilla pod
4 egg yolks
100g caster sugar
chocolate cookies (crushed)

To Serve

fresh seasonal Manx berries

Method

For the Cheesecake

Crush the digestive biscuits, then melt the butter and add it to the crushed biscuits.

Place the mixture into a 25.5cm/10 inch cake tin and leave in the fridge overnight. Mix the cream cheese and sugar in a bowl and whip the double cream separately. Melt the chocolate and then add the orange juice and the grated orange peel.

Put the gelatine leaf into cold water and soak it.

Next add the whipped cream to the cheese mixture. Add the gelatine into the chocolate mixture and allow it to cool it down.Mix the cheese and chocolate mixtures together until they acquire a full, dark colour and pour this over the biscuit in the cake tin. Leave this to set overnight.

For the Cookies Ice Cream

Place the milk and cream in a saucepan. Split the vanilla pod lengthways and add to the mixture in the pan, and then cook over a low heat.

Once reaching boiling point, remove the saucepan from the heat and allow to simmer off the heat until cool.

Beat the egg yolks and sugar together. Strain the contents of the saucepan into the egg and sugar mixture and mix gently.

Put the mixture in a clean saucepan and gently cook this on a low heat for 5 minutes, until it sticks to the back of a mixing spoon. Cool down the mixture and rest in the fridge.

Cool the ice cream churner and, once cold, pour in the ice cream mixture and churn for approximately an hour (or per the manufacturer's instructions).

Once the ice cream starts to densify, add the broken cookies into it. Remove once churned and place in a plastic container in the freezer.

To Serve

Slice the cheesecake and arrange on a plate.

Using some crushed cookies as a base, place a ball of ice cream on the plate. Garnish with fresh seasonal Manx berries.

Titan

42, Broadway, Douglas
01624 613697
www.titanbroadway.com   titanbroadway@gmail.com

We are a small, family run restaurant situated in the heart of Douglas, providing a friendly service in vibrant and contemporary surroundings with culinary delights from our three chefs – Rick, Deano and head chef David – who between them have over 80 years of expertise.

We devise menus based upon our knowledge from all corners of the world, and we work hand in hand with local farmers, fishermen and artisan producers to create a truly unique taste experience.

We have a tantalising range of meat, fish and vegetarian starters from our Wild Garlic Mushrooms and Manx Slow-Cooked Glazed Short Rib, to our Manx King Scallops Thermidor.

Our signature dish – THE TITAN – is select cuts of prime Manx meats skewered and marinated in various ways and then chargrilled above special Himalayan coals. They are hung on our specially made stands above hand-cut skin-on fries, special artisan salad and served with dipping sauces.

To suit an array of palates our chefs also put together an ever-changing, locally and seasonally sourced specials menu ranging from our Beef Wellington to line-caught seabass and many other local delicacies.

For those with a sweet tooth Titan has homemade desserts found nowhere else, from our infamous Deanezze, speciality Broadway Fudge Creme Brûlée and our secret-recipe Salty, Extra Caramel and Toffee Cheesecake.

To accompany all of these great flavours we have a selection of locally produced beer, cider, juices and a wide choice of fantastic wines.

Team Titan are a group of passionate individuals who have come together for the love of food, drink and service. Our front of house team always wants you to have a brilliant night and our chefs are the same, therefore they always insist on using the utmost quality, fresh and locally sourced produce.

Chef Deano even forages for his own blackberries to confirm that they are perfectly ripe. He also has a keen eye for wild garlic at its best. We hope that the three dishes that have been published in the Island Kitchen cookbook can give you an insight into our chefs' minds to create your very own fabulous dinner party or a romantic meal.

Starter from Titan

Manx king scallop thermidor

serves 4

Ingredients

Manx Staarvey Farm pea shoots
Fynoderee Gin –Spring Edition
1 tbsp lemon juice
1 tbsp lime juice

Sauce

25g butter
1 good-sized banana shallot (finely diced)
2 garlic cloves (finely crushed)
200ml fish stock
100ml good white wine
110ml double cream
1 tsp English mustard
2 tbsp fresh parsley
juice of half a lemon
salt and freshly ground pepper to taste

Scallops

a knob of butter
200g fresh baby leaf spinach
12 good-sized Manx king scallops (prepared, roe optional)
olive oil
salt and freshly ground pepper to taste

To Serve

12 half shells
200g fresh Parmesan cheese (finely grated)
small bunch of parsley

Method

First prepare your plates with pea shoots as an under garnish, as this will hold the shells steady on the plates. Add a good glug of gin into a jug and add the tablespoon of lime and the tablespoon of lemon to the gin. Put this to the side as this is used to flambé the scallops later.

For the Sauce

To make the sauce place the butter in a pan over a medium heat and add the finely diced shallot and crushed garlic. Cook until softened but do not over-brown.

Next pour in the fish stock and the white wine and reduce by two-thirds. Add the double cream and bring to the boil, reduce by a half, stirring occasionally. Now add the mustard, parsley and lemon juice. Season to taste with salt and freshly ground pepper.

Leave to cool to room temperature as this will thicken and coat the scallops better.

To Prepare the Shells with Spinach

Lay out 12 scallop shells on an oven tray. Place a knob of butter in a pan on a medium heat and add the spinach. Season with black pepper and cook until wilted. Distribute the cooked spinach evenly between the shells.

To Seal the Scallops

Put the scallops in a tray, lightly season and coat with olive oil. Place a skillet pan on a high heat and when hot, place the 12 scallops one at a time into the pan

When the 12th scallop is in, turn the 1st placed one over and continue this until the 12th is turned.

Throw in the Manx gin and flambé. When the

flames die down, remove the scallops in the same order as placed into the pan.

To Serve

Place 1 scallop into each of the earlier prepared shells, on top of the spinach.

Place a teaspoon of thermidor sauce on top of each scallop then add a pinch of Parmesan onto each one.

Put under a pre-heated hot (250°C) grill until golden – this will only take minutes so do not leave unattended!

Take out when golden and arrange on the prepared plates.

Sprinkle with chopped fresh parsley and serve.

Main course from Titan
Individual beef wellingtons
serves 4

Ingredients

Wellingtons

4 x 8oz fillet steaks
olive oil
1 good-sized banana shallot
350g fresh mushrooms
1 knob of butter
2 sprigs of thyme
150ml white wine
30g Parmesan cheese (grated)
good quality pre-rolled puff pastry sheets
200g quality Brussels pâté
1 egg (beaten)
1 egg yolk
salt and pepper

For Port and Shallot Jus

2 shallots
160ml port
160ml red wine
1 thyme sprig
1 bay leaf
1 sprig of rosemary
800ml high-quality beef stock
salt, pepper and sugar to taste

To Serve

sprigs of rosemary

Method

For the Wellingtons

Preheat oven to 220°C/200°C fan oven/gas 7

Coat the steaks with olive oil and season with salt and pepper. Then heat up a skillet pan until smoking hot and seal all sides of each steak in the hot pan.

Place the steaks on a warm tray, allowing them to rest.

Next, finely dice the shallot and chop the mushrooms into small cubes. Place the butter in pan over a medium heat, add the shallot, mushrooms, thyme sprigs and white wine. Cook until the liquid has been absorbed and has a paste-like consistency. Remove the thyme sprigs and stir in the Parmesan cheese.

Cut the pastry into approximately 18cm / 7 inch squares, spread the pâté onto the centre of each piece of pastry and place a spoon of the mushroom mix on top of the pâté.

Place the cooled steaks on top of the mixture and lightly brush the edges of the pastry squares with the beaten egg. Bring the opposite corners of the pastry squares together and pinch tightly to seal.

Next, place each wellington on a baking tray, ensuring the pâté mixture is on the top.

Brush with egg yolk and score lightly in opposite directions without breaking the pastry.

Place into the pre-heated oven and cook for 20–25 minutes until the pastry is golden brown. Remove from the oven and leave to rest.

For the Port and Shallot Jus

For the jus, dice the shallots very finely, add the port, the wine and the herbs bring to the boils and simmer, reducing this by a half. Add the beef stock and reduce by half again.

When ready, discard the herbs and season to taste.

To Serve

When the wellingtons have rested for 5 minutes place on a warm plate.

Place the jus in jug on the plate and garnish each wellington with a sprig of rosemary.

THE ISLAND KITCHEN VOLUME TWO

Dessert from Titan
Chocolate orange deanezze
serves 4

Ingredients

Brownie

160g butter
100g chocolate pellets
100g plain flour
45g cocoa powder
90g mini eggs
50g marshmallows
4 eggs
150g sugar

Mousse

175g dark chocolate (70% cocoa)
2 tbsp golden caster sugar
4 egg whites
2 sheets gelatine
284ml double cream
orange zest
orange essence

To Serve

good quality vanilla ice cream
strawberries
physallis
ice cream wafers
chocolate orange segment
icing sugar

Method

For the Brownie

Cut the butter into small cubes, place in a bowl and add the chocolate pellets. Fill a small saucepan ¼ full of hot water and sit the bowl on top (taking care not to allow the bowl to touch the water). Put the saucepan with bowl on top over a low heat until the chocolate is melted, stirring occasionally.

Cover loosely with cling film and leave the mixture to one side to cool to room temperature. Preheat oven to 200°C/180°C fan oven/gas 6

Take a 20cm square tin and line the base with baking parchment. Tip the flour and cocoa powder through a sieve, together, into a bowl. Chop the mini eggs and marshmallows into small pieces and leave to one side.

Next break 4 eggs into a large bowl, add 150g of sugar and whisk until creamy and doubled in volume.

Pour the cooked chocolate mixture over the egg and sugar mix and fold together with a rubber spatula until the colour is molten, dark brown. Add the flour and cocoa powder mix and fold in gently, then stir in the mini eggs and marshmallows.

Pour the mixture into a baking tin and level out with a spatula. Bake in the preheated oven for 25 minutes and check – if it is wobbly place back in for a further 5 minutes. The top should have a shiny, papery crust.

Leave the brownie in the tin until cold then tip out of the tin and chop into small chunks.

For the Deanezze Mousse

Fill a small saucepan ¼ full of hot water, place 175g of dark chocolate into a bowl and sit this on top of the saucepan (again not touching water) and melt, stirring occasionally.

In the meantime, whisk sugar and egg whites to a stiff peak.

Melt the gelatine sheets in 100ml of boiling water.

Next warm the cream up to 60°C, then put cream and gelatine into the chocolate mix, whilst whisking vigorously. Fold the chocolate mixture into your egg whites and add orange zest and essence to taste.

To Serve

Take 4 large wine glasses and lay the brownie and mousse mixture alternatively into the glasses until you are 1cm from the top. Leave to set for approx. 2 hours in the fridge.

To serve add a scoop of quality vanilla ice cream, 1 strawberry, 1 physallis, 1 ice cream wafer and a chocolate orange segment.

Dust with icing sugar to finish.

L'Experience

Summerhill, Douglas, IM2 4PL
01624 623103
www.lex.co.im

Bonjour mes amis, if you look closely at the bottom of Summerhill Road you will notice a little slice of France.

Nestled between the red and blue tablecloths are the owners of this establishment – Michael runs the kitchen and Belinda is the Front of House. Married couple Michael and Belinda met at catering college, both their fathers were chefs and owning a restaurant was their dream from the beginning. After catering college Michael served in the Royal Green Jackets in the British army and Belinda worked in various catering roles within schools and restaurants.

L'expérience meant a great deal to Michael and Belinda as Michael had worked there as a boy. They bought L'expérience in 2009 and have never looked back; they boast the best French onion soup this side of the channel.

Away from the hustle and bustle of town, L'expérience host many events in the restaurant. They arrange themed evenings such as 'Allo Allo' and support charities by having special fundraising evenings. They also work with the schools on the Island and do French tasting classes: the owners feel that teaching children about cooking is a valuable life skill.

As cooking is such a tremendous part of Michael and Belinda's lives, everything at L'expérience is cooked to order and the staff pride themselves on being as hospitable as possible and will bend to anyone's needs or preferences. So come and visit the heart of France in the Isle of Man, you will never want to go back!

Au Revoir, à bientôt!

Starter from L'Experience
Steak tartare
serves 4

Ingredients

100g Harrison & Garett beef fillet (finely chopped)
2 gherkins (finely chopped)
1 tsp capers (rinsed, drained and finely chopped)
1 shallots (finely chopped)
½ tsp Dijon mustard
few drops Tabasco sauce
½ tsp Worcestershire sauce
salt and freshly ground black pepper

To Serve

4 bread crisps of dark rye or
pumpernickel bread
1 free-range Gelling egg yolk

Method

Place the chopped beef, gherkins, capers and shallot into a bowl and mix well. Add the mustard, Tabasco sauce, Worcestershire sauce, salt and freshly ground black pepper and mix well.

To Serve

Spoon the steak tartare mixture onto a slice of plain or toasted dark rye or pumpernickel bread.

Make a small dent in the top of the tartare and top with a fresh egg yolk. Eat immediately.

Main course from L'Experience
Lobster thermidor served with chips

serves 1

Ingredients

1 x 750g Devereau lobster

Sauce

25g salted butter
1 shallot (finely chopped)
275ml fish stock
55ml white wine
110ml double cream
½ tsp English mustard
2 tbsp parsley (chopped)
½ lemon, juice only
salt and freshly ground black pepper

Chips

2 large floury potatoes
(cut into 1.5cm thick long chips)
vegetable oil, for deep-frying

To Serve

20g fresh Parmesan cheese
(grated)

Method

How to Cook the Lobster

Boil a large pan of salted water. Place the lobster into the boiling water; allow the water to return to a boil and leave to simmer for 15–20 minutes, depending on the size of the fish. If you are in doubt as to whether or not it is cooked, carefully push a carving fork or skewer into the middle of the shellfish; if the skewer or fork is hot to your lips the lobster meat is cooked.

Drain the lobster and rinse with cold water to remove any excess protein on the shell and allow to cool.

To Prepare the Lobster

Place the lobster on a chopping board with the head facing you. With a sharp robust knife, cut down into the shell in the middle of the head (there is a recess half way down). Cut down towards the head of the fish, separating the 2 sides.

Repeat the process this time cutting towards the tail of the fish, ending up with 2 halves. Remove the pouch, which is located close to the head; this is the only inedible part of a lobster.

Break the claws from the body and remove the meat using a rolling pin or other object to crack the shell.

For the Sauce

To make the sauce, place the butter into a pan over a medium heat. Add the shallots and cook until softened. Pour in the stock, wine and double cream and bring to the boil. Reduce by half, stirring occasionally. Add the mustard, herbs, lemon juice and season to taste.

For the Chips

To make the chips, heat the vegetable oil in a deep-fat fryer to 140°C (CAUTION: Hot oil is very

dangerous. Do not leave unattended). Carefully drop in the chips and cook for 5–6 minutes or until just tender, without colour.

Remove using a metal slotted spoon. Turn the heat to 190°C. Place the chips back into the hot oil and fry for 3–4 minutes or until golden and cooked through. Remove using a metal slotted spoon and drain on kitchen paper.

Season to taste and serve alongside the lobster.

To Serve

Spoon the sauce over the lobster meat. Sprinkle with Parmesan cheese and grill for 3–4 minutes until golden brown. Serve with the seasoned chips.

Dessert from L'Experience

Chocolate fondant

with raspberry ripple ice cream and raspberry coulis

serves 5

Ingredients

150g butter (melted, plus extra for greasing)
150g dark chocolate (melted)
7 whole eggs
80g caster sugar
120g plain flour
cocoa powder (to dust the ramekins)

To Serve

100ml raspberry coulis
5 scoops raspberry ripple ice cream

Method

Preheat oven to 220°C/200°C fan oven/gas 7
Using a glass bowl, mix the melted butter and melted chocolate together.

Mix the eggs and sugar together in a separate bowl, whisking them until they form a white foam. Add the egg mix to the chocolate mix, and sieve in the flour gradually a spoonful at a time, while mixing slowly with a whisk or a wooden spoon. Leave the mixture in the fridge for half an hour to rest.

Using soufflé ramekins, coat the inside of the

dishes with a little melted butter and dust with cocoa powder. Divide the mix between the 5 ramekins. Place the ramekins in the oven, and cook for 8 minutes at 200°C fan oven/gas 7. After 8 minutes, remove the fondant from the oven and leave to rest for 1 minute to set.

Place a spoonful of raspberry coulis on each plate and hit with a spoon, to create a splattered effect.

Take the fondants out of the ramekins and serve with Davison's raspberry ripple ice cream.

New Manila

Queens Promenade, Douglas, Isle of Man IM2 4NH
01624 660600
newmanila.co.uk

Building on many years of experienced and unrivalled reputation, we are one of the best authentic Thai restaurants on the Isle of Man.

New Manila serves Thai cuisine prepared according to ancient recipes, from the family recipe books of proprietor Melody Crosby, with a focus on how the flavours and textures of premium-quality ingredients interact together. Customers can either enjoy their meal in our fully licensed restaurant or use our takeaway service when preferring to eat at home.

All our food is cooked to order by our three talented Thai chefs, who pride themselves on serving only the finest and freshest ingredients cooked to a consistently high standard.

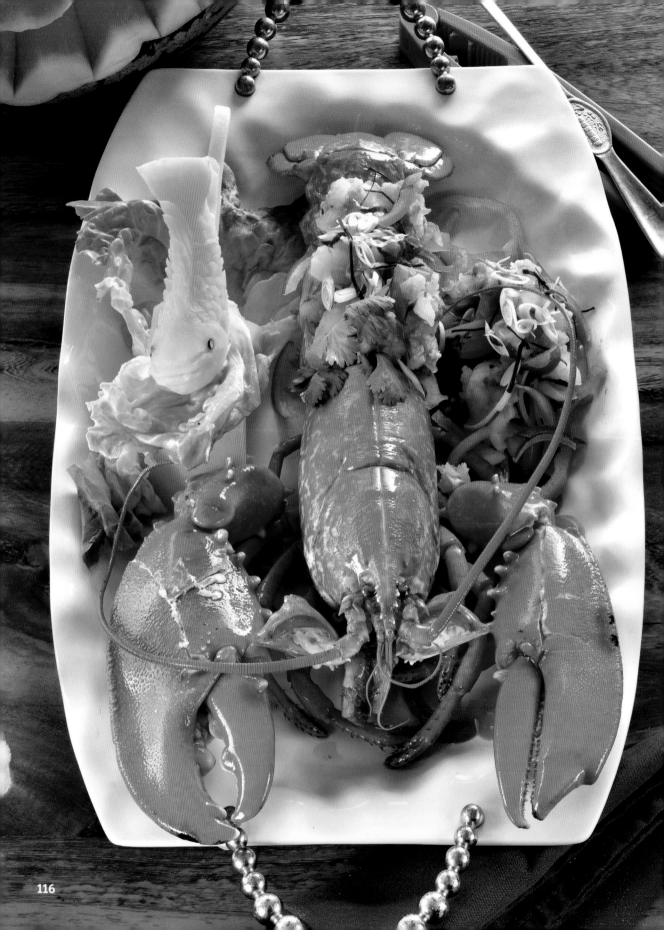

Thai lobster salad

serves 2

Ingredients

Lobster

1 small or medium whole lobster

Thai Spicy Sauce

2 long red chillies
3 birds-eye chillies
5 garlic cloves
1 coriander stalk
1 tsp palm sugar
4 tsp of lemon juice

Sauce

2 tsp fish sauce
3 tsp lemon or lime juice
1 tsp palm sugar
Thai spicy sauce (prepared earlier)
2 stalks lemongrass (thinly sliced)
1 small red onions or shallots (thinly sliced)
1 red pepper (thinly sliced)
1 green pepper (thinly. sliced)

Method

For the Thai Spicy Sauce

Place all the ingredients in a blender and mix well. Set aside to use later

To Prepare the Lobster

Wash the lobster.

With a sharp knife, sever the head at the base of the neck and cut off both claw arms.

Discard the carapace (body shell) and legs. Cut the soft underside of the tail lengthwise with scissors, then crack the hard shell so you can remove the tail meat.

Place the claws and tail meat on the grill about 10–13cm (4–5in) from the flame and grill for 5–6 minutes. Turn the claw and tail meat over and grill on the other side. The cooked lobster will be bright red when done.

When cooked put the lobster on a plate and set aside.

For the Sauce

In another bowl add the fish sauce, lemon or lime juice, palm sugar and the Thai spicy sauce prepared earlier.

Stir them all together and set aside

To Serve

Add the lemongrass, red onions, red and green peppers to the bowl of ingredients and mix well. Pour over the grilled lobster and serve.

Main course from New Manila

Grilled Manx rack of lamb

in massaman curry sauce

serves 2

Ingredients

Massaman Curry Paste

5 garlic cloves (peeled)
1 or 2 fresh long red chillies (or dried chillies)
1 piece galangal
1 stalk of lemongrass (minced)
1 tsp ground coriander
½ tbsp ground cumin seeds
a pinch of nutmeg
½ tsp cinnamon
a pinch of ground cloves
2 tsp fish sauce
1 tsp palm sugar

Sauce

1 can coconut milk
1 cup of lamb stock
4 new potatoes (peeled and pre-cooked)
1 cup unsalted peanuts or cashew nuts

Lamb

1 rack of lamb trimmed (with the excess fat removed)

To Serve

Crispy onions (optional)

Method

For the Massaman Curry Paste

Place all the paste ingredients in a food processor or blender and process well.

For the Sauce

To make a sauce rather than a paste, add up to 1 can of coconut milk, depending on how thick you prefer your sauce. Set the paste and coconut milk in a pot and bring to boil for at least 15 minutes.

Add the lamb stock, new potatoes and peanuts.

For the Manx Lamb Rack

Heat the grill

Place the Manx lamb rack fat side down on the grill. Flip the meat and continue cooking the rack of lamb for an additional 15 minutes.

To Serve

Plate the Manx rack of lamb and pour the curry sauce over the meat.

Sprinkle with crispy onions.

Dessert from New Manila
Thai pandan pancake
serves 1

Ingredients

Pancake

100g pandan leaves (extracted)
300g Laxey self-raising flour
1 egg
150g cornflour
50ml milk
oil

Filling

1 egg
50ml condensed milk
50ml double cream
300g white sugar
25ml coconut milk
175ml rice flour
100g pandan leaves (extracted)

To Serve

cream or ice cream

Method

For the Pandan Pancake

Cut the pandan leaves up and blend them with a little water. Drain the pandan water into a jug, removing the remaining bits of leaf with a strainer. Place the jug of pandan water to one side for later.

Mix the self-raising flour, egg, cornflour and milk in a large bowl. Add the pandan water, a small amount at a time, until the consistency is creamy.

Put a little oil onto a piece of kitchen towel and wipe this round the surface of a frying pan and put on to heat.

Add half a ladle of mixture to the frying pan – this should be a thin layer.

Keep the pancake turning while it cooks for a few minutes.

For the Filling

Start by beating the egg in a mixing bowl, ensuring that the egg mix is smooth. Gradually add the condensed milk, double cream, sugar, coconut milk, rice flour and pandan water. Continue to beat all the ingredients in the bowl until they are all blended.

Place the mixture in the top of a double boiler or a heatproof bowl set over a saucepan of simmering water (do not let the glass touch the water), cook, stirring occasionally until blended, about 2–3 minutes.

Place the filling into the pandan pancake.

To Serve

To present it, roll the pancake. If desired serve with ice cream or cream.

NEW MANILA - DESSERT

Regency Hotel

Queens Promenade, Douglas, IM2 4NN
01624 676000
www.regency.im

Located on the ground floor of The Regency Hotel, the elegant restaurant and its intimate bar are ideal surroundings in which to experience excellent food.

A combination of traditional and modern, in muted tones with panoramic sea views, oak-panelled walls and generously-spaced immaculately dressed tables, the restaurant can cater for up to 60 diners and is a wonderful location for a wedding. The Regency Hotel, also boasts a supremely comfortable exclusive private dining room for up to 20 guests where privacy and intimacy is guaranteed, and menus can be created to suit each individual customer's taste.

Carl takes full advantage of all the wonderful produce the Island has to offer and works closely with local growers and suppliers to guarantee that the produce is at its seasonal best. The menu changes daily, offering dishes to suit all tastes from hotel residents to local people wanting to celebrate that special occasion. From the homemade crisps and breads to start your meal, to the petits fours of truffles and fudge, all the food is produced by the kitchen team.

Whatever the dish you choose it is always geared around quality ingredients and attentive cooking.

From bespoke menus and eight-course tasting menus to Manx fillet steak, all tastes and requirements are catered for and are all treated with the same care and attention.

The food is complemented by an exciting modern wine list featuring New World wines as well as some European classics.

With his wife Renee at the Front of House, and her attention to detail working alongside her friendly and professional team, this restaurant is very much becoming a destination for both the discerning traveller and local alike.

Duo of mackerel

serves 4

Ingredients

Boulangère Potato

50g butter
2 large onions
(peeled and thinly sliced)
1kg potato
(peeled and thinly sliced)
4 sprigs fresh thyme
400ml fish stock
salt and pepper

Horseradish Cream

100g crème fraiche
20g horseradish (freshly grated)
1 tsp Dijon mustard
juice of ½ lemon
seasoning

4 large mackerel (filleted and pinned)
20g butter
100g wild garlic
olive oil for frying
lemon juice
salt and pepper

Method

For the Boulangère Potato

Preheat oven to 160°C/gas 3

Melt the butter in a pan, add the onions and slowly cook without colour on a low heat. Cover the base of a suitably sized ovenproof dish with sliced potatoes. Next cover the potato with a thin layer of the cooked onion.

Sprinkle thyme leaves over the onion and season with salt and pepper then arrange another layer of potatoes over the onion.

Repeat the process with layers of onion and potato until all the onion is used. Finish with a layer of potato.

Pour the fish stock over the potatoes until it is just visible below the top layer of potato. Cover the dish with tinfoil and place in the preheated for approximately 45 minutes.

Check the potatoes are cooked with a knife, allow to cool and place in the fridge until needed.

For the Horseradish Cream

Place all the ingredients into a mixing bowl and gently fold them together so that they are all incorporated. Check for seasoning and adjust if necessary. Place in a small container and keep in the fridge until required.

For the Mackerel

Cut the mackerel fillets in half, giving you 8 pieces, season and place 4 pieces into a smoker. Heat up the olive oil in a frying pan, place the remaining mackerel fillets in the pan, skin side down, and fry for approximately 2 minutes until the skin is crispand season the mackerel with a little lemon juice.

In the meantime, melt a little butter in another pan and cook off the wild garlic.

If a smoker isn't available both pieces of mackerel can be cooked in a pan.

To Serve

Place the wild garlic at the bottom of the plate and the boulangère potato at the top.

Place the fried mackerel fillet on the garlic and the smoked mackerel on top of the potato. Dot the horseradish cream around the plate.

Main course from Regency Hotel
Manx rib of beef
serves 2

Ingredients

Dauphinoise Potato

1.5kg potatoes
500ml double cream
1 garlic bulb
salt and pepper

1 x 800g rib of beef on the bone
2 bunches of cherry tomatoes on the vine
200g spinach (washed)
salt and pepper
fresh nutmeg (grated)
olive oil
butter

Method

For the Dauphinoise Potato

Preheat oven to 160°C/gas 3

Peel all the garlic cloves and coarsely chop, then place in a pan with the double cream and slowly heat. Allow to simmer but do not boil. Season well

Next peel and thinly slice the potatoes, then place them in layers in a suitable ovenproof dish.

Remove the garlic from the cream and pour the cream over the potatoes so that it lightly covers the surface.

Place in an oven at 160°C and cook approximately 40 minutes until the potatoes are cooked and the top is golden in colour.

For the Beef

Season the rib and using a hot pan or grill, cook to the desired degree.

Season the tomatoes, coat with a little olive oil and place in the oven for 3 minutes. Melt a little butter in a pan and add the spinach. Cook until wilted and season with salt, pepper and a little nutmeg.

To serve the beef, remove the bone and cut into 6 equal sized slices, arrange on a plate with the grilled tomato.

Dessert from Regency Hotel

Manx mess

serves up to 8

Ingredients

Burnt Butter Ice Cream

170g unsalted butter
300ml milk
300ml double cream
6 egg yolks
125g light brown soft sugar

Honey Crème Brûlée

250ml full-fat milk
250ml double cream
100g egg yolks
75g caster sugar
75g Manx honey

Buttermilk Panna Cotta

3 leaves gelatine
300ml milk
75g caster sugar
1 vanilla pod
300ml buttermilk

To Serve

local strawberries
egg meringues
milk meringues

Method

For the Burnt Butter Ice Cream

Place the butter in a frying pan and heat gently until the butter begins to foam and turns a nut brown colour. Whisk well and pour the butter into a container then set aside.

Put the milk and the cream in a pan and slowly bring to the boil. In the meantime, whisk the egg yolks and sugar together until they form a light cream consistency.

Pour the hot milk and cream over the egg and sugar mixture and mix well until all the sugar has dissolved. Return the mixture to the heat and cook slowly until it thickens and can coat the back of a spoon. Mix in the melted butter, pass the mixture through a fine sieve into a clean container and cool. Place the mixture into an ice cream maker and churn.

For the Honey Crème Brûlée

Preheat oven to 120°C/gas ½

Put the milk and cream into a pan and slowly bring to the boil. In the meantime, whisk the egg yolks, sugar and honey together until thick and light in colour. Next, pour the boiled milk and cream into the egg mixture and whisk well.

Sieve the 'custard' into a suitable container, Place in a water bath and cook in the oven until the brulees are set.

Buttermilk Panna Cotta

First soak the gelatine leaves in cold water. Put the milk and sugar in a pan, split the vanilla pod, scrape out the seeds and add to the milk then slowly bring to the boil. Squeeze out the excess water from the gelatine leaves and mix in the hot milk until they have dissolved completely.

Whisk in the buttermilk, sieve the mixture into a suitable container and place in the fridge to set.

To Serve

In a large bowl, place a scoop of ice cream, panna cotta and brûlée mixture. Liberally garnish with strawberries and meringues.

Seven Kingdom

Banks Circus, Douglas, IM1 1JE
01624 620232
www.sevenkingdomdistillery.com

Our distillery, bar and restaurant are located inside a former mechanic's garage on the North Quay in Douglas, and the bar is where you really feel the former usage of the site.

Sympathetically refurbished to retain much of the original character, the bar at Seven Kingdom is a great place to relax after a day's work, or enjoy a night out sampling our own spirits (made metres away!), our cocktail menu, or our carefully selected collection of high quality drinks from around the world.

Our highly trained and knowledgeable bar staff can talk you through our selections and guide you towards a wonderful drinking experience with us.

Head Chef Damien and Sous Chef Mat work tirelessly to produce some of the best food available on this beautiful Island, our consistent number one 5-star position on TripAdvisor is testament to this.

We operate both an à la carte and a bar menu, sourcing the finest, fresh seasonal ingredients from local suppliers, to create a comprehensive, modern and above all delicious offering.

Starter from Seven Kingdom

Kipper pâté

on lemon and dill scones with a fennel salad

serves 8

Ingredients

Lemon and Dill Scones

350g Laxey Mill self-raising flour
½ tsp bicarbonate of soda
85g Isle of Man Creamery butter
½ lemon (zested)
10g dill (chopped)
284ml carton Isle of Man Creamery buttermilk
a little milk to glaze (optional)
a good pinch of salt

Kipper Pâté

600g Manx kipper fillets
300g good quality cream cheese
10g dill (chopped)
½ lemon (zested and juiced)
a good pinch of cracked black pepper

Fennel Salad

selected salad leaves
fennel (finely sliced, fronds included)

Method

For the Lemon and Dill Scones

Preheat oven to 220°C/200°C fan/gas 7

Mix the flour, bicarbonate of soda and salt in a bowl. Add the butter, cut into small pieces and rub with your fingertips until the mixture resembles fine breadcrumbs. Next tip in the lemon zest, dill and buttermilk and mix lightly and quickly to form a soft dough. Knead very briefly, then roll out to 4cm thickness and cut into eight 5cm rounds. Place a little apart on a baking sheet (no need to grease), brush the tops lightly with milk or leftover buttermilk and bake for 12–15 minutes until risen and golden. Put on a rack to cool completely.

For the Kipper Pâté

Put the kipper fillets, cream cheese, dill, lemon zest and juice, and a good pinch of black pepper into a food processor. Pulse until you have a smooth pâté consistency. Transfer into a suitable container and chill until ready to use.

To Serve

Gently warm the scones through in a low oven. Either quenelle the pâté or place into small ramekins, garnish with a handful of the salad leaves and finely sliced fennel, and serve with the warmed scones.

Main course from Seven Kingdom
Seafood gratin
serves 4

Ingredients

Velouté Sauce

150g Isle of Man Creamery butter
150g Laxey Mill plain flour
150ml white wine
600ml good quality fish stock, hot
salt and cracked black pepper

Gratin

2.4kg (600g per dish) fresh mixed seafood
(e.g. salmon, smoked haddock, king prawns and
white fish)

Gratin continued

1 bunch spring onions (chopped)
400g mature Manx Cheddar (grated)
200g fresh breadcrumbs (or 50/50 fresh/panko
breadcrumbs)

To Serve

samphire (wilted)
pea shoots
lemon wedges

Method

For the Velouté Sauce

Melt the butter in a large saucepan over a low heat. Once melted, add the flour and whisk together to form a roux. Cook the roux for 1 minute then whisk in the white wine, stirring well to avoid lumps. Have the hot fish stock ready in a separate pan. Once the wine has been incorporated, whisk in the fish stock, again stirring constantly to avoid lumps forming. The velouté sauce may seem thin when the stock is added, it will thicken. Season to taste. Turn the heat up to medium and cook the sauce for 10 minutes, stirring constantly to avoid sticking. Remove from the heat and pour into a suitable container, leave to cool then refrigerate.

The sauce will keep for 3–5 days stored in an airtight container.

For the Gratin

Preheat oven to 220°C/200°C fan/gas 7
4 x 20cm/8" good quality pie/gratin dishes
Prepare the seafood and cut your fish into 2–

2.5cm chunks. Arrange in the bottom of each gratin dish, leaving small gaps to allow the sauce to evenly coat the fish. Sprinkle over a handful of spring onions. Using a wooden spoon, loosen the velouté sauce in its container until it is a spreadable consistency. Spread evenly over the fish and spring onions, ensuring there is just enough sauce to cover.

Next sprinkle 100g of cheese and 50g of breadcrumbs over each dish. Place in the centre of the preheated oven for 12–15 minutes until bubbling and brown on top and the fish breaks apart easily when tested with a fork.

To Serve

Top the dishes with wilted samphire, a handful of pea shoots and a lemon wedge

Chef's note: *Pick seafood that is fresh and seasonal. Add mashed potato before sprinkling over the cheese and breadcrumbs to make a fish pie.*

Dessert from Seven Kingdom

Chocolate fondants

with mixed fresh berries and vanilla ice cream

serves 6

Ingredients

105g good quality dark chocolate (74% solids)
105g Isle of Man Creamery unsalted butter
2 whole eggs
53g caster sugar
21g Laxey Mill plain flour
4g Isle of Man Creamery unsalted butter (softened)
12g cocoa powder

To Serve

your preferred fresh, seasonal berries homemade or shop-bought coulis or chocolate sauce.

Method

Preheat oven to 220°C/200°C fan/gas 7
6 x 114g dariole tins

Combine the chocolate and butter in a heatproof bowl over a pan of hot water until they have melted together. Meanwhile, whisk the whole eggs together, slowly incorporating the caster sugar until light and fluffy (the lighter and fluffier the mix, the taller and lighter your fondant will be). Add the chocolate and butter mix to the egg and sugar mix, then add the flour and whisk until completely combined.

Line the fondant tins by using a pastry brush to spread the softened butter up and around each tin, up to the lip. Spoon 2g of cocoa powder into each tin, tip and rotate the powder around the tins until they are well coated. Tip out the excess powder. Fill the tins three-quarters of the way up to the top. Place on a baking tray in the oven for 7 minutes.

When cooked carefully tip each fondant out and serve immediately, as the fondant will continue to cook if left in the tin and may collapse if left out.

To Serve

Tip the fondant on to a plate, serve with a selection of fresh, seasonal berries and a scoop of vanilla ice cream.

Chef's note: *Pick whatever fresh seasonal berries you like, serve with a homemade or shop-bought coulis or chocolate sauce. Instead of ice cream try fresh custard or even pouring cream.*

PORTOFINO

Portofino

1 Bridge Road, Quay West, Douglas, IM1 5AG
01624 617755
www.portofino.im

Mario Ciappelli arrived on the Isle of Man at the age of 14, starting his career at the Palace Hotel before returning to Italy to complete his training, gaining his Diploma in Hospitality and Catering in Turin.

After working on cruise ships for three years, travelling around the world and the Caribbean, he returned to the Island to settle down and in 1989 opened his first restaurant, Ciappelli's.

Six years later the time was right to move on and he opened The Max Restaurant at the King Edward Bay Golf and Country Club in Onchan before retiring for a few years to concentrate on family life. Moving back into his career Mario, and his brother Enzo,

opened La Cucina Restaurant in Bucks Road, Douglas.

Purchasing the site for a new restaurant at the prestigious Quay West, Mario put his heart and soul into his next new venture, Portofino, which opened late in 2010. Located in a fantastic position looking out over the stunning Douglas marina, the modern building houses a stylish interior, which creates a relaxed atmosphere for fine dining.

Using the highest quality local produce Mario creates mouth-watering dishes that are sure to impress.

Portofino specialises in the finest seafood, Mediterranean and international cuisine.

Starter from Portofino

Leek and lobster terrine
with pickled cucumber
serves 8

Ingredients

Terrine

1420g leeks (roughly 6 regular-sized leeks)
4 x 680g lobsters

Pickled Cucumber

1 large cucumber
1 tsp sea salt
1 tbsp caster sugar
1 tbsp white wine vinegar
½ tsp coriander seeds
a few sprigs of dill

Method

For the Terrine

Double-line a terrine mould with cling film.

Remove the tops of the leeks and braise in vegetable stock until soft, remove from stock and chill.

Cook the lobsters for 6 minutes in rolling boiling water, remove from the shell leaving the tails whole and set aside.

Peel the leeks, layer by layer, and line the terrine mould, leaving an overlap, then start filling the terrine with the rest of the leek, lining the bottom by about 1.25cm/½ inch. Next add the meat from 2 lobster tails and 4 claws plus any excess meat. Repeat the layering process until the terrine mould is full, seasoning each layer with salt and pepper as you go. Refrigerate for 12 hours.

For the Pickled Cucumber

Trim the ends from the cucumber, cut in half widthways and spiralise into thick ribbons.

Combine the rest of the ingredients, then toss the cucumber in the pickle mix. Leave for 15 minutes and then squeeze out any excess moisture.

Main course from Portofino

Crispy braised belly pork

king scallops, curried parsnip purée, pak choi

serves 4

Ingredients

Belly Pork

3 carrots (roughly chopped)
1 large leek (roughly chopped)
1 head of celery (roughly chopped)
2 white onions (roughly chopped)
2 garlic bulbs (roughly chopped)
a few springs of rosemary and thyme
500ml white wine
2 ltr vegetable stock
2kg belly pork
Salt

Curried Parsnip Purée

1 large white onion (diced)
1 tbsp mild curry powder
1 ltr vegetable stock
500ml double cream
1kg parsnip (peeled and roughly chopped)

To Serve

3 king scallops (mussel and roe removed)
pak choi
vegetable stock

Method

For the Belly Pork

Preheat oven to 180°C/gas 4

Roast the vegetables, garlic and rosemary and thyme in a deep baking tray or dish. Add the white wine and vegetable stock, then place the belly pork, skin side up, in the dish, cover in baking parchment and tinfoil. Bake at 180°C for 12 hours. Remove from the oven, drain excess stock and chill.

Preheat oven to 220°C/gas 7

When the pork is chilled, score the skin, rub generously with salt, return to oven at 220°C for 20 minutes until there's a nice crispy crackling.

For the Curried Parsnip Purée

Sauté the onions, add the curry powder then add a little stock to cook the spices. Next add the rest of the stock, cream and parsnips and boil until soft. Remove from the stock, place in a food processer and blend to a thick smooth purée.

To Serve

Sauté the king scallops in a smoking hot pan until golden brown on each side. This will take about 1 minute per side.

Cut the pak choi in half and braise in vegetable stock until soft. Season and roast in the oven.

Dessert from Portofino

Chocolate soufflé

serves 4

Ingredients

Crème Patisserie

1 tbsp plain flour
2 tsp caster sugar
½ tsp cornflour
1 whole egg
1 egg yolk
4 tbsp milk
4 tsp cream
25g good quality chocolate (in pieces)
1 tbsp cocoa powder

For the Ganache

4 tbsp double cream
50g dark chocolate
1 tbsp cocoa powder

Soufflé

6 egg whites
85g of caster sugar
25g unsalted butter
chocolate (finely grated) or cocoa powder

Method

For the Crème Patisserie

Mix the flour, sugar and cornflour together. Put the egg plus the yolk in a mixing bowl, beat in half of the flour mix to create a paste, then add rest of the flour and mix well.

Boil the milk and cream, then remove from the heat, add the chocolate and cocoa powder beat until smooth with no lumps. Gradually add the hot chocolate to the flour mix, return to the pan on a medium heat, stirring constantly until you have a smooth thick paste. Leave to chill.

For the Ganache

Warm the cream in a pan, just before it starts to boil, remove from the heat, add the chocolate and beat constantly to create a velvety texture. Add the cocoa, mix well and allow to cool.

To Assemble the Souffles

Preheat oven to 190°C/170°C fan oven/gas 5
Grease ramekins with butter and coat in grated chocolate or cocoa powder.

With an electric mixer, whisk the egg whites to a soft peak. Gradually add the sugar as you are mixing until you create stiff, firm peaks. Mix the crème patisserie and ganache in a large mixing bowl, then fold in the egg whites.

Spoon the mixture into ramekins and bake in the preheated oven for 15–17 minutes.

Serve immediately.

Coast

18–22 Loch Promenade, Douglas, IM1 2LX
01624 698800
www.coast.im/

Coast Bar & Brasserie is part of the Claremont, officially the highest-rated hotel on the Isle of Man, unique in having achieved 4-Star Gold status and offering its guests a refined excellence in both hospitality and cuisine.

Located on the promenade at the heart of the Island's capital, Douglas, and situated adjacent to the Island's government buildings, business district, retail area and ferry terminal, the Claremont provides an ideal base for both business and leisure.

Our philosophy is simply 'Excellence as Standard' with opulent rooms that delicately balance modern aesthetics, luxurious comfort and the connectivity requirements of the modern-day traveller. With complimentary superfast Wi-Fi throughout the property, welcoming staff, business support and conference services, and featuring the beautiful Coast Bar & Brasserie, the Claremont provides the perfect location.

Centrally located to the Loch Promenade at the heart of Douglas, with stunning panoramic views across the bay and out to sea, Coast Bar & Brasserie is renowned as a first-class restaurant, where guests can choose from a selection of exquisite dishes full of local Manx produce. Featuring all-day dining and a friendly attentive service, Coast is the perfect location to enjoy breakfast, a two-course express lunch, luxury afternoon tea, or an à la carte dinner.

Starter from Coast

Manx queenie linguine

serves 4

Ingredients

250g linguine
150g shallots (sliced)
3 garlic cloves (sliced)
150g sun blushed tomatoes
300g Manx queenies
100ml white wine
2 pinches of chilli flakes
oil for frying

salt and pepper

To Serve

8 basil leaves (julienned)
Parmesan cheese (grated)
lemon wedges
sprigs of rocket

Method

First, cook the pasta until it's al dente, chill and leave to one side.

In a large non-stick frying pan, sauté the shallots and garlic until they become a golden colour, then add the sun blushed tomatoes and keep cooking, and stirring, until they are nice colour. Take off the heat and set aside on a tray.

Next clean the pan and put back on the heat. Get the pan smoking hot, oil and season the queenies then place in the pan and sauté for about 2 minutes, making sure the pan stays on the heat and that you

get a nice colour on the queenies. Take them out of the pan and put to one side.

Put the white wine into the pan and deglaze by scraping the queenie juice off and into the wine. Reduce by half, add the shallot and tomato mix to the wine in the pan and add 2 pinches of chilli. Next, add the pasta and queenies to the pan and toss until hot.

To Serve

Serve with the basil, sprinkle with grated Parmesan cheese and serve with a lemon wedge and sprigs of rocket.

Main course from Coast
Herb-crusted chump of Manx lamb
with grilled veg and red wine jus
serves 4

Ingredients

Crust

10g mint
10g flat-leaf parsley
10g rosemary
100g breadcrumbs (dried)
50g fresh Parmesan cheese

Grilled Vegetables

2 aubergines (sliced)
3 courgettes (sliced)
2 red onions (cut into wedges)
2 red peppers
2 yellow peppers
10 cooked new potatoes (cut in half)
2 sprigs of rosemary (chopped)
4 garlic cloves (sliced)

Grilled Vegetables (continued)

olive oil
salt and pepper

Lamb

4 x 200g chumps of Manx lamb
2 tbsp Dijon mustard
oil for frying

Red Wine Jus

200ml red wine (Bordeaux or a Côtes du Rhône)

To Serve

pea shoot sprigs
rosemary (chopped)

Method

Preheat oven to 230°C/210°C fan oven/gas 8

For the Crust

For the crust put all the herbs, breadcrumbs and Parmesan into a food processor and blitz until mixed together. It should look green in colour. Put to one side for later.

For the Grilled Vegetables

Grill all the vegetables by first putting a griddle pan or a large frying pan on your stove. Keep all your sliced vegetables separate.

Oil and season your sliced aubergine, put on the hot griddle pan or frying pan until you have a nice colour on each side, then take off the heat and repeat with the courgettes and red onions.

Put the whole peppers onto a roasting tray, sprinkle with oil and season, then roast in the oven for about 10–15 minutes, or until they have a dark colour all over them. Take out of the oven, place in a bowl and cover with cling film to cool down for about 15 minutes. Next take off the cling film, peel the peppers, de-seed and cut them up.

Add the peppers to the rest of the vegetables, add the halved, cooked, new potatoes, chopped rosemary and sliced cloves of garlic, and leave to one side.

For the Lamb

Place a frying pan large enough to accommodate the 4 chumps of lamb onto the stove. Get the pan hot, then place the lamb in the pan and fry until a nice colour, sealing in the juices.

Next place the lamb on a tray, fat side down, in the oven for 7 minutes then turn so the fat side is facing upwards. Brush the lamb with Dijon mustard, place the lamb in the breadcrumb mix and then put back in the oven for a further 7 minutes.

Take out of the oven and leave the lamb to rest for 10–15 minutes.

For the Red Wine Jus

While the lamb is cooking, put the red wine into the pan used for frying the lamb and deglaze by scraping all the juices into the wine, continue cooking and reduce the red wine by three-quarters.

To Serve

Drizzle more olive oil onto the vegetable and potato mix and put it in the oven to heat up. Once the mix is hot to the touch, place neatly on the centre of a large plate, slice the lamb and put on top of the vegetables. Heat up the red wine reduction and pour over the lamb.

Garnish with a pea shoot sprig and chopped rosemary.

Dessert from Coast
Molten toffee pudding
serves 4

Ingredients

Toffee molten centre

200g soft brown sugar
150ml cream

Sponge

150g unsalted butter
(softened, plus extra for lining moulds)
150g soft brown sugar
2 large free-range eggs
½ tsp vanilla extract
150g plain flour

To Serve

Manx vanilla ice cream

Method

For the Toffee Molten Centre

Place the brown sugar and cream into a pan, put on a low heat and stir to melt the sugar. Once melted, turn up the heat and boil for 3 minutes or until thick.

Put to one side and leave to cool until cold and set.

Once set, roll into nut-sized balls and place in the fridge.

For the Sponge

Preheat oven to 210°C/200°C fan oven/gas 7

Put the butter and sugar into a mixing bowl and whisk at full speed until pale and fluffy. Add your eggs one by one, then add the vanilla extract and finally the flour. Make sure it is all mixed properly, then turn off and put to one side.

Take four 7.5cm Dario moulds and line them with soft butter, making sure there are no gaps. Fill the moulds to three-quarters full with the sponge mixture, and then poke a hole with a wet finger into the mixture. Place a ball of the caramel mix into the centre of the hole in each mould (reserving any left over) and cover with the last of the mix. Put the moulds into the centre of the oven and cook for 15 minutes.

To Serve

Melt the leftover caramel in a pan, and serve with the puddings and some Manx vanilla ice cream.

1886 Bar, Grill and Cocktail Lounge

6 Regent Street, Douglas, IM1 2EA
01624 611886 www.1886bars.com

1886 Bar, Grill and Cocktail Lounge is a majestic four-storey building located in the heart of Douglas on Regent Street, on the old Post Office site.

We have an elegant 125-cover restaurant with skylights and sloping ceilings located on the mezzanine level; there is also a large factory-glass window looking down onto the bustling bar below. On the ground floor there is a large 250-capacity bar with an amazing 15-metre-long art deco bar frontage, high ceilings and original structural steels and brickwork. Our bar has a huge selection of draught beers, bottled lagers and beers, and extensive cocktail and wine menus, all at reasonable prices. We have a very strong sports and entertainment offering on this floor too, including DJs and live bands that will keep you going until the very late hours at the weekend should you so desire!

On the second floor we have an exclusive and design-led cocktail lounge, which holds 125 people. This has a New York loft-style feel with high ceilings, huge windows and exposed, original, Victorian red brickwork, this is primarily aimed at the more discerning customer who wants amazing cocktails and entertainment in a stylish environment.

To top it off, on the fourth floor is 'Tanners Loft' which is a complete floor dedicated to fulfil the needs of the customer who requires a private hire/corporate hire space for up to 125 people.

Our food offerings and menus have been designed very much with the customer in mind. This may sound obvious, but we have focused on giving the customers the types of dishes that we know they want and desire. The management team and owners have a huge amount of local knowledge, running large and successful businesses, this has allowed us to design a menu that will leave the customer struggling to pick which dish they want off the extensive menu. Our head chef is an ex 'Isle of Man Chef of the Year' and as such he and his large brigade of chefs are dedicated to sourcing the best and freshest local ingredients – every single dish we make is cooked from fresh ingredients and made on-site, fresh to order for our guests. The service from the staff is friendly, welcoming and warm, and we want the guests to feel relaxed and able to enjoy their experience here fully.

Our wine and cocktail list has been designed to match the foods perfectly and also offer the customer a large and varied choice. We have a choice of over 40 wines and 20 cocktails and 4 bars that are fully stocked with an extensive offering of speciality spirits and liqueurs. Obviously we have a huge selection of specialist gins to suit the most discerning gin connoisseur too!

1886 Bar, Grill and Cocktail Lounge – the complete hospitality offer on the Island; the hub for quality food, drinks and good times on the Isle of Man.

THE ISLAND KITCHEN VOLUME TWO

Starter from 1886
Salmon, Manx crab and Parmesan croquettes
with pea shoots, cherry tomato and edamame bean salad, peri-peri mayonnaise and a jalapeno and balsamic jam

serves 6

Ingredients

Croquettes

1 x 20g red chilli (de-seeded)
½ stick lemongrass
300g salmon fillet
white wine (a splash)
600g Manx potatoes (pre-boiled and cooled)
10g coriander (finely chopped)
30g Parmesan cheese (grated)
200g local fresh crab meat
egg
flour
200ml milk
100g dry breadcrumbs (make your own if possible)
olive oil
salt and pepper

Salad

50g radish
50g spring onion

Salad (contined)

150g mixed cherry tomatoes
50g pea shoots
100g edamame beans
50g beetroot
French dressing

Chilli Jam

100g white onion
50g jalapenos
50g demerara sugar
75ml aged balsamic vinegar
100g tomato purée
salt and pepper

Peri-peri Mayonnaise

150g mayonnaise
150g peri-peri sauce (we make our own but *Nando's* is an ideal replacement)

To Serve

pea shoots
lime zest

Method

For the Croquettes

Preheat oven to 180°C/gas 4

Finely chop the chilli and lemongrass and add to the salmon fillet on a baking tray. Season and add a splash of white wine and olive oil, then put into the preheated oven to cook the salmon for 8–10 minutes. Once the salmon is cooked, remove and allow to cool.

In the meantime take the pre-boiled potatoes and add to a mixing bowl. When the salmon is cooled, flake the salmon into the bowl and add the remaining ingredients from the tray to the potato mix. Next add the finely chopped coriander,

grated Parmesan and the crab meat, season accordingly. Gently mix until the mix is firm and holds together, mould into whatever shapes you fancy. Add to a fresh tray and put to the fridge for half an hour.

Lightly pane the croquettes in flour, egg and seasoned breadcrumbs and when ready shallow fry until golden brown, usually 90 seconds to 2 minutes dependent on the size of your croquettes.

For the Salad

Thinly slice the radish and spring onion, then a quarter of the cherry tomatoes and add to a bowl with the pea shoots and beetroot. Very lightly dress with French dressing.

For the Chilli Jam

Finely chop the white onions and jalapenos and add to a pan with the sugar and balsamic vinegar, reduce for 20 minutes on a medium heat, until all nicely caramelised. Remove from the heat and stir in the tomato purée and season to your taste.

Serve when cold, if there's extra put in to a jar and save until next time.

For the Peri-Peri Mayonnaise

Simply mix together mayonnaise and peri-peri sauce.

To Serve

Plate up as you wish and garnish using more pea shoots and lime zest.

Main course from 1886

Slow braised local Loaghtan lamb shank

in a wild Manx herb crust, beetroot and goat's cheese creamed potatoes,
carrot and parsnip dauphinoise and a chorizo infused jus

serves 4

Ingredients

Lamb Shank

4 good quality lamb shanks
300g chorizo
600g carrots (roughly chopped)
300g leeks (roughly chopped)
800g white onions (roughly chopped)
3 garlic cloves
20g rosemary
20g thyme
4 tbsp plain flour
200g tomato purée
375ml red wine
olive oil
lamb or chicken stock
salt and pepper

Herb Crust

100g crusty bread
20g rosemary
20g thyme
20g chives
20g parsley

Jus

3 tsp redcurrant jelly
chorizo slices
juices and vegetables left from the cooking
of the lamb shanks

Dauphinoise

500g carrots
500g parsnip
150g onion
1 garlic clove
10g thyme
500ml Isle of Man Creamery double cream
20g Dijon mustard
50g Parmesan cheese
oil
a knob of butter
salt and pepper

Creamed Potatoes

1kg Manx potatoes
50g Isle of Man Creamery butter
50ml Isle of Man Creamery double cream
50g goat's cheese
salt and pepper

Beetroot Purée

200g peeled / prepped beetroot
10ml balsamic vinegar
5g chives
salt and pepper

continued on page 160

Slow braised local Loaghtan lamb shank

Method

For the Lamb Shanks

Preheat oven to 160°C/gas 3

First, trim and tidy up the shanks and season with salt and pepper. In a deep tray or pot, seal off the seasoned shanks on a medium to high heat in olive oil, until nicely browned.

Put the shanks to the side and add the chorizo and roughly chopped carrots, leeks, onions, salt and pepper to the pan. When the chorizo and vegetables are slightly sautéed and have become browned, add the garlic, rosemary, thyme, flour and tomato purée. Stir and add the red wine, reduce slightly and remove from the heat (This will become the base for the jus later).

Stand the lamb shanks, bone up, in between the vegetables in the tray, top up with lamb or chicken stock, so the shanks are completely covered, add a lid and put into the preheated oven for 2.5–3 hours. Until the meat starts to fall from the bone.

For the Herb Crust

Using a food processor blend together the crusty bread and mixed herbs until they turn into a fine crumb.

Remove the shanks from the tray, reserving the vegetables, chorizo and liquid, and roll the shanks lightly in the crust. When ready return to the oven for 5 minutes to brown off slightly, just before serving.

For the Jus

Using the vegetables, chorizo and liquid mix from the lamb shanks, return to boil on a high heat in a pan. When it starts to reduce and thicken, strain the jus, keeping the chorizo, add back to the heat, adding redcurrant jelly and the chorizo slices to finish.

For the Dauphinoise

Preheat oven to 190°C /170°C fan oven/gas 5

Thinly slice carrot and parsnips using a mandolin.

Heat oil in saucepan, thinly dice the onions and add to the pan with a good pinch of seasoning and sautee until soft. Add a knob of butter, garlic and thyme and stir. Next add the cream, Dijon and Parmesan and reduce slightly, then strain.

Remove from the heat, and layer the parsnips and carrots in a dish, adding the infused cream every few layers. When finished sprinkle a few Parmesan shavings on top, make sure the layers are firmly pushed down together.

Bake in the preheated oven for 30–45 minutes until the vegetables are soft and golden brown on top.

For the Creamed Potatoes and Beetroot Purée

Peel the potatoes and cut into cubes. Add to boiling salted water for 15–20 minutes.

While cooking add the prepped beetroot to a food processor with a dash of balsamic and water and blend into a purée.

When the potatoes are cooked, drain and mash together with the butter, cream and beetroot purée. Stir through the crumbled goat's cheese, chives, taste and season.

Plate up as you wish and enjoy.

Dessert from 1886

Honeycomb and white chocolate cookie s'mores
with a raspberry, wild berry gin and vanilla cream, topped with a salted caramel sauce
serves 6

Ingredients

Honeycomb

200g caster sugar
5 tbsp golden syrup
2 tsp bicarbonate of soda
butter (for greasing the trays)

Salted Caramel Sauce

90g Isle of Man Creamery butter
200g soft dark brown sugar
120ml evaporated milk
1 tsp salt

Cookies

170g Isle of Man Creamery butter (melted)
220g brown sugar
100g white sugar
1 egg yolk
15ml vanilla essence
250g plain flour

Cookies (continued)

335g cocoa powder
2g baking soda
pinch of salt
honeycomb
white chocolate chunks
salted caramel sauce
marshmallow

Raspberry Cream

200ml Isle of Man Creamery double cream
1 tbsp icing sugar
50g raspberries (smashed)
½ vanilla pod (de-seeded)
½ shot Fynoderee Summer Fruits gin

To Serve

fresh berries
icing sugar

Method

For the Honeycomb

First butter a baking tray. Mix together caster sugar and syrup in a saucepan on a gentle heat, and heat until the sugar dissolves. Turn up the heat and keep stirring until the mixture becomes a caramel colour. Remove from the heat and stir in the bi-carb until the mixture is foaming. At which point add to the tray.

Allow to cool for 1 hour and the honeycomb will be ready to use.

For the Salted Caramel

In a saucepan, add the butter, sugar and evaporated milk and allow to gently simmer. When melted remove from the heat and add the salt. Salt to your own taste.

For the Cookies

Preheat oven to 165°C/gas 4

Line a tray with baking paper. Cream the butter and sugar together and add the egg and vanilla essence. Next sift in the flour, cocoa powder, baking powder and a pinch of salt and mix well.

Break in pieces of honeycomb and white chocolate and fold together.

Portion the mixture in to appropriate cookie sizes on the tray and bake for around 15–20 minutes. Place on a wire rack, put some salted caramel sauce and the marshmallow in between two cookies, allowing the marshmallow to gently melt.

Best served straight away while gooey and warm.

For the Raspberry Cream

Whisk the cream until soft peaks are formed and sift in the icing sugar, smashed raspberries, vanilla seeds and a splash of gin. Fold together making sure the cream holds and serve.

To Serve

Put it all together and garnish with some fresh berries and icing sugar.

Jean-Pierre's Bistro

Court Row, Ramsey, IM8 1JS
01624 819839 www.jeanpierresbistro.com

Since opening six years ago, Jean Pierre's has become synonymous with high-quality, leisurely Manx dining with a French twist. Well-established in the Old Post Office in Ramsey, the restaurant has become a firm favourite for discerning diners wanting to enjoy a relaxed, friendly atmosphere while sampling some of the finest food the Isle of Man has to offer. Owner, Carol Charsley, is proud to support the Island's producers and believes in the importance of creating beautiful dishes made with the freshest, home-produced ingredients.

Customers at the Bistro are highly valued: everyone at Jean-Pierre's strives to create the perfect dining experience. Their philosophy is to stand on the Three Legs of Mann – service, quality of food and ambience.

Jean Pierre's is proud to be an establishment that puts its customers first. Team members are dedicated and take pride in giving outstanding service – warm, friendly, efficient and professional. Attentive and friendly front of house staff ensure that the dining experience is one to be savoured. All three kitchen staff are born, raised and have been educated in Ramsey, and the front of house staff are all local too!

Newly appointed head chef, Tyler Livesey, Isle of Man Chef of the Year 2019, has been in the industry since the age of 16: studying at the University College Isle of Man for five years, and joining Jean-Pierre's four and a half years ago as chef de partie. He then became sous-chef, and was appointed head chef at the beginning of August 2019. His first major task, after getting to grips with his new responsibilities, was putting himself forward for Chef of the Year, which he went on to win.

Tyler's winning dish of succulent, locally-sourced saddle of goat with bonbons of goat's leg, and a tamarind and pomegranate jus, was beautifully plated to represent the Three Legs of Mann, in keeping with the restaurant's philosophy, reflecting the importance of Manx cuisine and tradition. You can recreate the winning recipe in the comfort of your own home as it features in the recipe section following.

Our selected starter reflects the French twist inherent in the Bistro's menu: a beautifully, soft, light twice-baked soufflé with the sharpness of a well matured Cheddar. Dessert is a French classic: a refreshing lemon brûlée, with a crisp, caramelised top to perfectly complement Tyler's crumbly, homemade shortbread.

Tyler is supported in the kitchen by two new members of staff – chef de partie, Reanne Beattie, and trainee sous-chef, Andrew Brandrick.

Reanne has been chef de partie since the beginning of 2019, dedicated to her craft she attends the University College, when not in the Bistro, to progress her culinary skills. Andrew is mastering the skill of creating sumptuous starters and giving support in the kitchen. He too attends University College when not at Jean Pierre's.

Carol also runs a delicatessen within the restaurant building. Imported cheeses and charcuterie, along with complementary bottles and biscuits, can be purchased, allowing customers to create a little of the Bistro's ambience for themselves.

Providing relaxed high-quality dining with a top-class service, in an elegant and warm atmosphere, is important at Jean Pierre's Bistro, and is something everyone is proud to attain.

Starter from Jean-Pierre's Bistro

Twice baked cheese soufflé

made with Abergavenny mature Cheddar

serves 2

Ingredients

50g plain flour
50g butter (plus extra to grease ramekins)
150ml full-fat milk
45g Abergavenny mature Cheddar (plus extra grated for cheese glaze)
1 tsp parsley (chopped)
1 tsp horseradish sauce

1 large egg
double cream to glaze
salt and pepper

To Serve

creamy garlic velouté

Method

Preheat oven to 150°C/130°C fan oven/gas 2

Start by greasing two ramekins so they are ready for the mix.

In a heavy-based saucepan create a roux by combining the flour and butter on a low heat to make an almost sandy texture. Once the roux is made add your milk to the same pan and continue to stir until its thick enough to coat the back of the spoon.

Next add the cheese, parsley and horseradish and cook the mix out until the cheese has fully melted. After the cheese has melted separate the egg, keeping both the yolk and the white.

Add the yolk to the cheese mix, stir to incorporate and take off the heat to cool slightly.

While the mix is cooling, place the egg white in a mixing bowl and whisk to a stiff peak.

When the white is whisked, fold half at a time into the cheese mix, slowly and softly to prevent knocking back the air too much from the whites. After folding, season the mix according to personal taste.

Divide the mixture between both ramekins and cook in a tray with water (bain-marie style) for 30 minutes, turn the tray and cook for a further 30 minutes.

Chef's note: *A good indicator to show if the soufflés are ready is when they are golden brown on the surface of the soufflé, and fairly firm/slightly spongy to touch when you press the top.*

Once the soufflés are ready, take them out of the oven and allow to cool. When they are cool enough, demould onto a tray, pour some double cream over the top of each soufflé and scatter the cheese you grated earlier for the glaze.

To Serve

To finish, cook the soufflés in the oven for 7–8 minutes, look out for the soufflé swelling out a little on the tray and the cheese glaze having a nice colour.

Plate up with your preferred garnishes or sauces. We highly recommend a light and creamy garlic velouté to accompany your soufflé.

Main course from Jean-Pierre's Bistro

Hay-roasted back saddle of Manx goat

bonbon of goat leg filled with local goat's feta served with a root vegetable dauphinoise and a tamarind and pomegranate jus

serves 2

Ingredients

Hay-Roasted Back Saddle

2 back saddle cuts of goat
Manx rapeseed oil
sumac
200g hay
salt and pepper

Goat's Leg and Feta Bonbon

100g goat leg meat
120g goat's feta cheese
100g Manx potatoes
100g Laxey flour
2 Faragher's free-range eggs (beaten)
200g breadcrumbs (made from fresh bread)
oil for frying
salt and pepper

Root Vegetable Dauphinoise

100g parsnips
100g carrots
125g potatoes
1 onion
500ml double cream
2 tsp saffron
salt and pepper

Tamarind and Pomegranate Jus

1 shallot
3 garlic cloves
175ml red wine
250ml lamb stock
40g butter
40g flour
50g tamarind paste
half a pomegranate (deseeded)

Method

For the Hay-Roasted Back Saddle

Firstly marinate your goat back saddle with the rapeseed oil, sumac, and salt and pepper (overnight is strongly advised).

Preheat oven to 200°C/180°C fan oven/gas 6

Pan sear the marinated meat, and place in a parcel of tinfoil, with the hay inside the tinfoil too. Cook for 8–12 minutes, depending on your cooking preference, and allow to rest once cooked.

For the Goat's Leg and Feta Bonbon

Cook off your leg meat in a frying pan over a medium heat and allow to rest. Crumble the feta cheese in a separate bowl. Next prepare your potatoes and boil until soft, then mash and season to taste.

Once the mash is ready and the leg meat has cooled, dice the meat and add to the mash, followed by the crumbled feta, season to taste.

Roll your mix into 50g spheres and place in the fridge for 5–10 minutes to firm up. When ready, coat in flour, dip into the egg mix and coat with breadcrumbs.

Deep fry until a nice golden-brown colour is achieved all around the bonbon.

For the Root Vegetable Dauphinoise

Preheat oven to 200°C/180°C fan oven/gas 6

With a mandolin, slice all your root vegetables, potatoes and the onion.

Mix the cream with the saffron and add seasoning to taste.

Layer the vegetables in a 5cm/2-inch deep tray pouring a little cream in as you stack your layers.

Cover the tray with tinfoil and bake until the vegetables are cooked through and tender, about 30–40 minutes.

For the Tamarind and Pomegranate Jus

Sweat the shallots and garlic in a saucepan and add your red wine, reduce by half and add the lamb stock. Simmer for 10 minutes.

In a separate saucepan, create a roux by melting the butter and flour together.

Strain the stock mix into the roux, stirring, until the desired sauce consistency is met and the flour is cooked out, then add the pomegranate seeds and simmer for a further 10 minutes.

When the flour is cooked out, strain the seeds out of the sauce and season to taste, adding a little tamarind at a time until the desired flavour comes through, tasting as you go.

Dessert from Jean-Pierre's Bistro
Lemon brûlée with homemade shortbread
serves 6

Ingredients

Lemon Brûlée

450ml double cream
5 eggs
100g sugar
50ml lemon juice (roughly 5 lemons)

Shortbread

225g butter
113g sugar
340g flour

To Serve

sugar

Method

For the Lemon Brûlée

Preheat oven to 120°C/100°C fan oven/gas ½

First warm up the double cream in a heavy-based saucepan. While the cream is warming, separate the eggs, keeping the yolks for this recipe and the whites if you plan to make any meringues at a later date.

Whisk the egg yolks and sugar in a bowl. After the egg and sugar is whisked, pour your warm cream into the egg mix and then proceed to add the lemon juice to taste.

Fill your brûlée dishes a couple millimetres below the rim and place in a tray, fill the tray half way up the brûlée dish with water and cook them 'bain-marie' style in the preheated oven for 30–35 minutes.

Chef's note: *a good way to indicate if they are done is to jiggle the brûlée dish gently and there should be a wobble in the centre of the mix, roughly the same diameter as a 2 pence coin.*

Once you know they are ready, allow to cool completely and leave in the fridge ready to serve.

For the Shortbread

Preheat oven to 200°C /180°C fan oven/gas 6

Combine all your ingredients in a mixing bowl, continuing to mix until the mixture starts coming together just past a thick crumb.

Once you achieve this stage finish by kneading the pastry, with minimal flour on the work surface, to a dough consistency.

Split the dough into 2–3 discs, wrap in cling film and allow to rest for a minimum of 8 hours in the fridge.

Once rested, removed from the fridge to slightly soften the dough and roll out so that the pastry is as thick as a pound coin.

Stamp out to your desired shapes and sizes onto a tray. Cook for 8–10 minutes until golden brown and leave to cool.

To Serve

Pour sugar over the brûlées and gently work around the dish until an even coating is achieved. Tip out any excess sugar and using a blowtorch, carefully begin to caramelise the top. If the sugar colours too quickly, move the blowtorch away from the dish and gently blow to cool the cooking process. Repeat until whole top of the brûlée has been evenly caramelised.

Vellika's

6 Bowring Road, Ramsey, IM8 2LQ
01624818241
www.vellikas.com

The owner of Vellika's, Jose Verananickal, moved to the Isle of Man from India in 2006, working with his brother-in-law before establishing his own restaurant in 2015.

Both he and his award-winning chef, Jiju Ravindranath, grew up in Kerala along the southern Indian coast. Local fishing, traditional cooking techniques and the abundance of spices and vegetables in the area have highly influenced their style of food.

Vellika's menu is inspired by not only the spices and rural cooking of South India, but also the Manx produce available on the Island, creating a brilliantly unique Indian cuisine and showing off the fresh fish and vegetables that the Isle of Man is famous for.

With a range of different dishes, from Chilli Garlic Manx Queenies to Vegetable Korma Malabar, Varutharacha Kozhi Curry, and their signature dish, Jhinga Tandoori Charminar, Vellika's also caters well for intolerances with wonderful Kallappam, soft gluten-free pancakes made with coconut and cumin seeds, a fantastic alternative to naan bread. With a traditional clay oven, they offer many different flavoured naans and wonderful grill dishes.

Starter from Vellika's
Chemmeen patties with cassava chips
serves 4

Ingredients

Chemmeen Patties

20g oil
40g shallots (chopped)
2 sprigs curry leaves
20g turmeric powder
20g chilli powder
20g ginger (chopped)
20g garlic (chopped)
300g prawns (cleaned and deveined)
300g cassava (cleaned and boiled)
breadcrumbs
oil for frying
salt to taste

Cassava Chips

400g cassava
oil for frying
salt to taste

Coconut Chutney

250g coconut (grated)
1 green chilli
50g roasted Bengal gram
salt to taste

Method

For the Chemmeen Patties

Heat the oil in a pan, then add the shallots and sauté well. Add the curry leaves, turmeric powder, chilli powder, ginger and garlic and then add the cleaned prawns. Sauté this until well cooked.

Add the boiled cassava and mix well with the prawns.

Make equal-sized balls make patties and dust with the breadcrumbs.

Deep-fry in oil and keep to one side.

For the Cassava Chips

Cut the cassava into batons and boil until tender. Deep-fry in a pan and keep to one side.

For the Coconut Chutney

Mix all the ingredients and blitz to a paste in a blender.

To Serve

Plate the chemmeen with the cassava chips and add chutney on the side.

Main course from Vellika's

Jhinga charminar
(seabass stuffed with prawns)

serves 4

Ingredients

4 seabass fillets
4 large king prawns (deveined tail on)
1 ltr fish stock (to poach)

Sauce

30ml oil
250g shallots (chopped)
20g ginger (chopped)
10g garlic (chopped)
2 sprigs of curry leaves
10g turmeric
20g chilli powder (hot)
200ml water
250g coconut (grated)
2 dried red chillies
2 flakes cocum (soaked in water)

Method

To Stuff the Seabass

Take the seabass fillets and wrap each one around a king prawn. Use a tooth pick to secure them. Poach in the fish stock and set aside.

For the Sauce

Heat the oil in a pan, add the shallots, ginger, garlic, curry leaves and sauté well.

Add the turmeric powder and the chilli powder, and sauté for one further minute then add 200ml of water and simmer.

Grind the coconut, ginger and the dried chillies to make a fine paste.

Add the paste into simmering water then add the cocum and continue to simmer.

To Serve

Place the seabass on a plate and pour the sauce on top. Serve hot.

Dessert from Vellika's
Rice hoppers with ice cream

serves 4

Ingredients

200g idli rice (or parboiled rice or sona masuri rice)
50g coconut (fresh, desiccated or frozen)
50ml warm water (to activate the yeast)
½ tsp dry yeast

2 tsp sugar
salt to taste

To Serve

your ice cream of choice

Method

Firstly, soak the idli rice for 5 hours.

Place the soaked rice and coconut in a blender, add water as required and blend to a smooth batter.

To activate the yeast, add the warm water, dry yeast and sugar to a large bowl and rest for 5 minutes.

Now transfer the blended batter into the yeast water, mix well and ferment the batter for 8 hours.

Mix the batter slightly and add salt as required and a little water if needed. The batter has to be a flowing consistency.

Pour a ladleful of rice hopper batter on to a medium hot pan and immediately rotate and spread.

Cover and simmer until the mixture is cooked completely (the steam created will help the hoppers to cook).

Finally, serve the rice hoppers with ice cream.

Milntown

Milntown, Lezayre, IM7 2AB
01624 818091
www.milntown.org

The Milntown Estate is a popular family-friendly visitor attraction which was the home of the powerful Christian family for more than 500 years. It was latterly owned by Sir Clive Edwards, whose family were wealthy Welsh foundry owners.

He loved the Isle of Man and bequeathed the Estate in Trust for the benefit of the Manx people. At the heart of the Estate, surrounded by 15 acres of mature woodland, is a splendid white mansion, whose crenulated walls look magnificent etched against a clear blue sky.

House tours are held throughout the season. Close to the house are flourishing flower gardens and a sunny and secluded walled garden, where fruit, vegetables and herbs are grown especially for the table. Set in the beautiful grounds of the Estate are three fabulous self-catering apartments available to book throughout the year.

Milntown Café is set in a light and spacious conservatory with wonderful views of the walled garden. The conservatory is an addition that perfectly harmonises with the main house. It is an ideal place for morning coffee, a hearty lunch after a garden visit or a relaxing afternoon tea.

The menu offers a wide selection of home-cooked seasonal dishes, cakes and desserts. There is also a children's menu. The delicious cakes, puddings and home-baked scones often use fruit such as apples and rhubarb from the garden.

The emphasis on using home-grown local produce is part of the ethos of Milntown Café, with its own kitchen garden just a stone's throw from where the food is prepared.

Milltown's Café and special events Head Chef Sean Maxwell has no difficulty offering a menu packed with fresh, seasonal ingredients, incorporating them into dishes from his experiences travelling the world.

Catering Manager Peter Duggan said: 'Our customers are enjoying our great tasty food and friendly service, all in a beautiful and relaxed setting. 'Many come in just for lunch but will stay to visit the gardens, after visiting the gardens they come back to the Café for tea and our fruity homemade scones or a delicious slice of cake, sometimes even taking them home as a treat for later.'

The garden team work closely with Head Chef Sean enabling him to create the day's menu and also helping with suggestions for the coming seasons. The specials board is dictated by what is seasonally available and always features leafy salads based on what can be plucked fresh from the garden, which is run using organic methods.

The three courses featured here include tomatoes, cucumbers, leeks and berries – all fresh from the garden – and many locally sourced ingredients but are easily replicated at home.

Starter from Milntown
Nori rolls
serves 2

Ingredients

450g sushi rice
3 tbsp of sushi rice vinegar
5 sheets nori
1 cucumber (deseeded and cut into strips)
1 bunch chives
1 ripe avocado (cut into wedges dressed in lime and sesame oil)

To Serve

60ml (¼ cup) Kikkoman's soy sauce
1 tbsp pickled ginger
1 tube of wasabi

Method

Wash the rice until the water runs clear, place in a pan roughly one-third rice to two-thirds water, place a lid on the rice and gently steam until all the water has evaporated. Do not overcook the rice it should be light and fluffy. Tip the rice into a large tray and sprinkle with the sushi vinegar, cool the rice down by fanning it.

When the rice is cool, place a sheet of nori on a bamboo rolling mat, shiny side down. Moisten your hands with cold water and place a handful of rice in the centre of the nori, spread it out in a thin layer to fill the sheet evenly, leaving a 2cm space at the top and bottom of your nori. Place 1 strip of cucumber, some chives and avocado across the centre of the nori, so they run the entire width of the sheet. Start rolling the nori from the bottom by gripping the nori and the bamboo mat and using the mat to help you make a tight roll.

Let the nori rest, seam side down, while you repeat the remaining procedure with the remaining rice and nori. You should have 5 rolls.

To Serve

Wet the blade of a sharp knife and cut the rolls into rounds about 2.5cm / 1 inch thick. Serve at room temperature.

You can vary the fillings. Most fresh fish would be suitable, but I prefer salmon and tuna. You can also top with fresh Manx crab or salmon caviar. If you don't like raw fish smoked salmon or tofu is also good.

Serve with soy sauce, wasabi and pickled ginger on the side.

Chef's note: *be gentle with the rice, use cold water on your hands this will help you spread the rice evenly*

Main course from Milntown

Chicken en croute

serves 6

Ingredients

2 tbsp olive oil
5 skinless chicken breast fillets (cubed)
4 tbsp white wine (optional)
2 medium leeks (chopped)
15g butter
1 tbsp plain flour
750ml milk

1 chicken stock cube
200g Manx mature Cheddar
3 puff pastry sheets
1 free-range egg (beaten)
flour for dredging
salt and pepper

Method

Heat 1 tablespoon of oil in a frying pan until hot. Cook the chicken until brown all over and then set aside.

Using the same pan, heat the remaining oil and add the wine, if using, then add the leeks and cook and stir until the leeks are tender and the wine has evaporated. Set aside.

Melt the butter in a large pot and stir in the flour to create a smooth paste. Gradually add the milk, stock cube and Cheddar stirring continuously until the sauce thickens.

Add the chicken and leeks to the pot and season with salt and pepper. Cover and simmer over a low heat for 5–10 minutes, then allow to cool and place in the fridge. The mixture has to be thick to allow you to wrap it in pastry.

Preheat oven to 200°C/180°C fan oven/gas 6.

Meanwhile, take 3 puff pastry sheets cut in half, so you have roughly six 18cm/7inch squares. Brush the top with the egg, this will help seal the pastry when baked.

Divide the chicken and leek mixture between the pastry, taking care not to overfill. You should have space around the outside edges. With your fingers, bring in the corners of the pastry so they overlap forming a parcel. Gently turn the individual pies over and lightly dip in flour, remove any excess flour and place on greaseproof paper.

Place the pies on an ovenproof tray. Decorate the pies with any pastry left over, I prefer pastry bows but this can be tricky.

Bake in the preheated oven for 15 minutes or until the pastry is puffy and golden. Remove from the oven and serve.

This goes well with a rich tomato sauce.

Dessert from Milntown

Bombe Alaska

serves 2-4

Ingredients

Sponge Base

3 free-range eggs
100g caster sugar
100g self-raising flour

Bombe

500g strawberries (halved)
25ml brandy
1 ltr Davidson's ice cream
6 egg whites
100g (½ cup) caster sugar

Method

For the Sponge Base

Preheat oven to 190°C/170°C fan oven/gas 5
Grease a 20cm or 23cm round cake tin.

In a medium bowl, whip together the eggs and caster sugar until fluffy. Fold in the flour. Pour the mixture into the prepared tin.

Bake for 20 minutes in the preheated oven, or until the top of the cake springs back when lightly pressed. Cool in the tin over a wire rack.

For the Bombe

Preheat oven to 240°C/220°C fan oven/gas 9

When your sponge is cool drizzle the berries with brandy and place on top of the sponge, forming a mound. Top this with ice cream forming a dome and place in the freezer.

Whip your egg whites and sugar until the mixture forms soft peaks.

Using a spoon cover the prepared cake with the meringue, forming soft peaks, making sure you cover all of the cake.

Immediately place in the preheated oven until golden. Remove and serve straight away.

Café Rosa

Glen Duff, Lezayre, Ramsey, Isle of Man
01624 816609
www.caferosa.org

Café Rosa Restaurant is an elegant little establishment nestled in a quaint countryside setting, just outside of Ramsey, in Lezayre Parish ('the Garden of the Island'). Drive through wrought iron gates into a private cark park and gardens, and you will find the restaurant. With an eclectic interior of antiques, paintings and traditionally dressed tables, it offers a warm atmosphere in which to unwind and savour a varied cuisine.

Café Rosa is renowned for its signature two-course set-price menus (including tea or coffee) offering an uncommonly wide choice of mains, with everything from grilled fish platters, duck, and vibrant salads right through to finest Ballavair Manx Sirloin. For a small corkage, diners may also bring their own wines.

The hand-peeled rustic chips, using potatoes sourced from St. Judes village, remain ever popular.

Undoubtedly the main attraction, however, is the Island's largest choice of 100% homemade desserts, each created by Rosa on-site using Laxey Glen Mill flour and local free-range eggs. Every dessert is beautifully presented with patterned sauce garnishes, chocolate tuiles and accompanied with Manx ice cream and cream.

Diners choose from an ample photographic dessert menu consisting of decadent creations such as feather-light pear and almond sponge, triple-layer fruit gateau, deep-base lemon meringue pie, crème caramels, and several fruit meringue towers.

Every Sunday the finest Manx lamb, beef, pork and a host of lighter and vegetarian options are offered alongside the prerequisite roast potatoes, Yorkshire puddings, stuffing and trimmings – making it a preferred destination for whiling away leisurely weekends amongst friends and family.

Proprietors Chef Bob and Rosa Phillips are amongst the Island's longest-serving restaurateurs, cooking and serving continuously since 1982 when they opened their first restaurant, the eponymous 'La Rosette' Restaurant in the south of the Island, in Ballasalla village. This fine-dining restaurant won UK acclaim, including listing in the Egon Ronay and Michelin Guides, receiving the prestigious Prix Armagnac Janneau for French cuisine.

Prior to moving to the Island, the couple met while working in various top London hotels on Park Lane, as both chef and front of house respectively. Chef Bob has also cooked for the royal family while a retained chef at Lancaster House, a St. James mansion owned by HM Government.

In 1995, the couple closed 'La Rosette' and opened Café Rosa in the beautiful Manx countryside, and while the fayre may be simpler these days, the same high standards and dedication to attentive service remain.

Diners can rest assured a warm welcome awaits in this delightful outpost of the Island's dining scene, a veritable magnet for the dessert fan and only open on the weekends.

Starter from Café Rosa
Country baked mushrooms
(champignons à la campagne)

serves 2

Ingredients

4 large flat breakfast or Portobello mushrooms
2 tbsp extra virgin olive oil
fresh parsley (chopped)
2 garlic cloves (sliced)
sprinkle of turmeric
sprinkle of mild paprika
2 local orchard apples

250ml white wine (or Manx Dry Cider, or Manx Elderflower Wine)
1 level tsp arrowroot or cornflour (mixed with a little water to dilute)
sprig of fresh fennel
sea salt and ground pepper to taste

Method

Preheat oven to 220°C/200°C fan oven/gas 7

Take the flat breakfast or Portobello mushrooms, place onto a deep baking tray, add plenty of extra virgin olive oil, chopped fresh parsley, sliced garlic cloves, and sea salt and cracked pepper to taste. Lightly sprinkle over the turmeric and mild paprika. Cook in the hot oven for approximately 10 minutes.

While the mushrooms are cooking, peel 2 local orchard apples, core and slice. Gently poach the apples in the white wine (or Manx Dry Cider, or Manx Elderflower Wine) with a little salt and ground pepper until softened. Remove and drain the sliced apple, placing to one side.

Thicken the cooking liquor with a small amount (1 tsp) of arrowroot or cornflour, diluted with a little cold water.

To Serve

Remove the mushrooms from the oven, place onto the middle of a serving plate, arrange the sliced apple around the sides, coat with the thickened liquor.

Garnish with a sprig of fresh fennel.

THE ISLAND KITCHEN VOLUME TWO

Main course from Café Rosa

Mixed fish platter
(fruits de mer)

serves 2

Ingredients

275g halibut steak (or fillet)
1 cod fillet (no bones)
1 haddock fillet (skin on)
275g salmon
2 small sea bass fillets
10 king prawns (shelled)
6 fresh mussels
4 fresh scallops

200ml extra virgin olive oil
sprinkle of turmeric
2 garlic cloves (or Manx wild garlic, optional)
sea salt and ground pepper to taste

To Serve

tartare sauce, hollandaise or parsley sauce
lemon wedges

Method

Preheat oven to 220°C/200°C fan oven/gas 7

From the fishmonger, procure your fish and shellfish. Ask the fishmonger to remove all small fine bones from your cod. Allow 5 shelled king prawns per person and use 6 fresh mussels or 4 fresh scallops to garnish. Divide each variety of fish into 2 pieces to form the selection per person.

Place the fish in a deep-sided baking tray, liberally pour over extra virgin olive oil to prevent sticking and to increase the aroma and flavour. Sprinkle on sea salt,

ground pepper, and a fine dusting of turmeric for colour.

Chop the 2 cloves of garlic (optional) or a sprig of Manx wild garlic, and place in-between the fillets. Place in the preheated oven for 10 to 15 minutes, depending on your oven type.

To Serve

When the fish is ready, remove from the oven and place on a preheated plate. Serve with tartare sauce, hollandaise or parsley sauce, and a wedge of lemon.

Dessert from Café Rosa

Rosa's dessert selection:

(assortiment de petits desserts): **profiteroles**

serves 8

Ingredients

300ml water
pinch of fine table salt
175g Isle of Man Creamery butter
350g Laxey Glen Mill self-raising flour (sifted)
8 large local free-range eggs
250g dark cooking chocolate
Manx double cream
(or Manx vanilla ice cream)

Method

Preheat oven to 200°C/180°C fan oven/gas 6

Place the water, salt and butter in a medium-sized saucepan and bring to the boil. Add the sifted flour, beat vigorously with a wooden spoon, turn the heat down to simmer and then continue to cook the paste for approximately one minute. Remove from the heat.

Place the paste in a food mixer, attach a beater implement, turn on to a low speed and add one egg at a time into the mixture, beating on a gradually higher speed towards the end.

Spoon the mixture into a large piping bag. Carefully pipe medium-sized dollops onto a parchment/greaseproof paper-lined baking tray. Place in the preheated oven for 15–20 minutes, again depending on your type of oven (with or without fan).

Take a small pan, add around 200ml of water, bring to the boil, and turn down to simmer. Place a large bowl over the pan, then add the plain cooking chocolate to the bowl and allow to slowly melt down. Dip the hot profiteroles into the chocolate, so that the tops are fully coated.

Allow to cool down, cut in half and pipe in Manx whipped double cream (with a little sugar, if desired) or fill with Manx vanilla ice cream, and pour over some hot chocolate sauce to serve.

These profiteroles make up part of Rosa's dessert selection. To create your own selection, such as that pictured opposite, why not make your own meringues, millefeuille and chocolate cakes to add to the plate.

Filbey's

Peel Harbour, Peel, IM5 1AR
01624 844144
www.filbeys.com

The Filbey family are so proud and honoured to be invited back into *The Island Kitchen* for volume two – hard to believe it's been four years since the first edition!

Our lifelong dream of having our own little restaurant in Peel has gone from strength to strength over the last seven years and we are still enjoying every minute of it.

The recipes we have put together for this book have been inspired by the fantastic local produce we have available to us on the Island, which is only getting better and better each and every year! We have listed just a few of the amazing suppliers that we get to work with and hope you enjoy trying their lovely produce as well.

The Isle of Man is such a magical place, we are so lucky to have our restaurant here and we look forward to welcoming you to Filbey's soon!

Starter from Filbey's

Local crab with lobster pâté
pink grapefruit and avocado mousse
serves 4

Ingredients

Lobster Pâté

1 Manx lobster
4 tbsp cream cheese
fresh parsley (chopped)
fresh dill (chopped)
1 lemon (juice and zest)

Avocado Mousse

1 avocado
1 tbsp fresh coriander (chopped)
1 lime

To Serve

1 cucumber
1 pink grapefruit
12 crab claws
Staarvey Farm micro herbs
lemon slices
salt and pepper

Method

For the Lobster Pâté

Bring a large pan of water to the boil and place the lobster in the pan for 8–10 minutes, depending on the size. When cooked run under cold water and once cool remove the meat from the tail and claws.

Add the lobster meat to a bowl with the cream cheese, chopped parsley and dill and the lemon juice and zest. Mix well, cover and refrigerate.

While the lobster pâté is in the fridge, prepare the avocado mousse.

For the Avocado Mousse

Chop up the avocado, season with salt and pepper, add the chopped coriander and lime juice then blend until smooth. Cover and refrigerate.

To Serve

Peel the cucumber lengthways into ribbons and trim to equal lengths. Lay your strips alongside each other, then spoon your lobster pâté into the middle section. Roll the cucumber to make a cylinder then slice into 8 equal sections.

Cut the pink grapefruit into small segments.

Chef's note: *There are so many ways to plate this dish so be creative...*

We recommend: Place 2 sections of your cucumber cylinder on each plate, add the crab claws around the plate, then spoon on a few drops of the avocado mousse and decorate with segments of pink grapefruit and Staarvey Farm micro herbs. Finish off with a lemon slice.

Main course from Filbey's

Manx pork loin

serves 4

Ingredients

4 pork loin steaks (from Ballahig Farm)
4 rashers local smoked bacon
a small log black pudding (from Tate's Butchers)
150g Close Leece Farm chorizo (diced)
olive oil for frying
a knob of butter
salt and pepper

To Serve

pea purée

Method

Preheat oven to 200°C/180°C fan oven/gas 6.

Season the pork loins with salt and pepper. Heat a splash of olive oil in a frying pan, once hot sear the pork loins until nicely coloured. Place the pork loins on a baking tray and put in the oven for 16–18 minutes.

While the pork is cooking, slice the bacon into small strips and cut the black pudding into cubes. For the final 5 minutes of cooking time, place the bacon and black pudding under a hot grill. When the pork is ready, leave to rest in the baking tray for 5 minutes, then remove the pork, add a knob of butter to the meat juices and add the chorizo, then keep warm on a low heat.

To Serve

Add a generous spoonful of pea purée to the middle of the serving plate. Slice the pork into strips and lay over the pea purée, top the pork with bacon and place the black pudding cubes around the plate. Finish off by spooning the chorizo butter over the top.

Dessert from Filbey's
Lime and Manx gin posset
serves 4

Ingredients

Posset

400ml double cream
4 limes (juice and zest)
4 shots Manx Gin
200g sugar

Shortbread

100g butter
50g caster sugar
150g Laxey Glen Mills flour (plus a little extra)
icing sugar

To Serve

whipped cream
raspberries
blueberries
edible flowers

Method

For the Posset

Add the cream to a saucepan and bring almost to the boil, then add the sugar, stirring until dissolved. Next add the lime juice, zest and gin. Leave to cool for around 20 minutes. Pour the mixture into your chosen serving dishes and leave in the fridge to set for at least 3 hours.

For the Shortbread

Preheat oven to 190°C/gas 5.
Beat the butter and sugar together until smooth, then stir in the flour to form a smooth paste. Sprinkle a little bit of flour onto the work surface then gently roll out the mixture until about 1cm thick. Cut into circles or fingers and place on a baking tray. Sprinkle with icing sugar and leave in the fridge for 20 minutes. Bake in the oven for 15–18 minutes then set aside to cool.

To Serve

Top the posset with a spoonful of whipped cream, then decorate with fresh raspberries, blueberries and edible flowers. Serve with shortbread on the side.

The Boatyard

The Boatyard Restaurant, Mariners Wharf, East Quay, Peel, IM5 1AR
01624 845470
www.theboatyardpeel.com

The Mowat family opened The Boatyard Restaurant in May 2013 just after one of the worst winters the Island had experienced in over 30 years, with the west side of the Island effectively severed from the east by heavy snowfalls. Situated in the beautiful seaside town of Peel, on the Island's west coast, the restaurant enjoys a prominent location on the town's historic East Quay with superb views overlooking the marina and traditional fishing harbour.

Known locally as Sunset City, visitors to Peel are awarded some of the Island's most sensational sunsets – weather permitting. Peel also boasts two beautiful beaches as well as a working harbour, ancient castle and historic town making it a popular attraction for families, day trippers, and couples.

Built on the site of a former shipbuilding yard, the restaurant's name 'The Boatyard' became an obvious choice as a way of maintaining a connection to the building's past and town's seafaring heritage. Continuing the coastal and seaside theme into the restaurant, the interior has been tastefully designed to bring out the playful side of this Manx seaside town with shades of blue, maritime décor and shipping flags.

During the day, the restaurant is a popular location for the many visitors, families and friends enjoying the rugged coastal paths, sandy beaches and winding lanes Peel have to offer. In the evening the mood changes as the evening draws in and the candlelit dining room creates a warm and welcoming atmosphere.

The Boatyard's menu reflects its coastal location and has been developed around our philosophy of using as many local ingredients and as much local produce as possible.

hrough an opening into the kitchen, Head Chef Iain McPhilimey and his team prepare dishes made fresh to order, adding to the overall theatre of dining at The Boatyard. Fresh local fish and seafood, much of which is sourced from boats arriving just a few hundred feet from the restaurant, features prominently across our menus with a variety of daily blackboard specials highlighting the catch of the day.

Sourcing local produce has been made a lot easier in the past few years as the Island has seen a growth in independent food and drink producers, many of which are now regular suppliers to our restaurant, including Staarvey Farm salad leaves and herbs, Peel smoked kippers and Manx lobsters from Niarbyl to highlight just a few within a few miles of the restaurant.

Our drinks menu also features many locally crafted beverages including artisan beers, Manx fruit juices and sparkling pressés from the Apple Orphanage, and Manx mineral water from the Green Mann situated just down the road in St Johns.

Queenie pancakes
Makes 9/10 approx

Ingredients

2 eggs
230g plain flour (Queen Flour)
330ml full-fat milk
20g butter (melted)
parsley (finely chopped)
¼ tsp salt

White Sauce

Makes 560ml (1 pint)
25g butter
25g flour
600ml full-fat milk
salt

400g Manx queenies (approx. 40g per pancake)
crispy bacon pieces (as many as you like)
Manx vintage Cheddar (grated)
(as much as you like)
oil for frying

Method

For the Pancakes

Mix the eggs, flour, milk and salt together in a bowl until lump free. Add the melted butter and chopped parsley and mix. Taste for seasoning. Check the consistency and if the mixture is too thick, thin using a little more milk.

Lightly grease a hot pancake/crêpe pan with vegetable oil and place over a high heat. Place two-thirds of a small ladle of pancake mix into the middle and swirl to cover the pan. Cook on both sides.

Lay the pancakes out to cool, stack, and cover in cling film. Refrigerate until needed.

For the White Sauce

Melt the butter in a saucepan. Stir in the flour and cook for 1–2 minutes.

Take the pan off the heat and gradually stir in one-third of the milk. Return to the heat and simmer, stirring, until all the milk is absorbed.

Repeat this process, stirring all the time, allowing the sauce to become thick and shiny before adding more milk.

When all the milk is added bring to the boil. Simmer gently for 8–10 minutes and season with a little salt.

To Serve

Preheat oven to 200°C/180°C fan oven/gas 6
Lightly sauté the queenies in a very hot pan with 1 teaspoon of oil.

Place a pancake onto an ovenproof tray, put a spoonful of white sauce in one corner, topped with the lightly sautéed queenies. Cover with a pinch of crispy bacon pieces, and half a tablespoon of grated cheese. Fold the pancake into 4 quarters (fold in half and half again). Turn the pancake over, so all the folds are underneath. Place 1 tablespoon of white sauce over the pancake and sprinkle with grated cheese.

Repeat with each pancake and place into the preheated oven for 5 minutes.

Main course from The Boatyard
Smoked haddock, leek and pea gratin
serves 6

Ingredients

white sauce (see queenie pancake recipe)
125g smoked haddock per person (cut into
approx. 2cm cubes)
500g leeks (sliced in rounds, washed and cooked
until soft)
350g garden peas (frozen)
350g Manx mature Cheddar (grated)

350g breadcrumbs
6 free-range eggs

Method

Preheat oven to 200°C/180°C fan oven/gas 6

Place the smoked haddock, leeks and peas in
an ovenproof dish, these can be made individually
or in one large family sized dish. Cover with white
sauce and sprinkle with grated cheese. Top with
breadcrumbs.

Cook in a hot oven until bubbling and the
breadcrumbs are golden brown, approx. 12
minutes

To Serve

Serve with a poached egg

Chef's note: *create the gratin using amounts
of the ingredients as you prefer.*

Dessert from The Boatyard

Coffee budino
makes approx 6

Ingredients

Coffee Brûlée

1200ml double cream
270g caster sugar
6 egg yolks
180ml coffee espresso

Italian Meringue

100ml water
400g caster sugar
200g egg whites

To Serve

Amaretti biscuits (crushed)
coffee ice cream (vanilla ice cream with a
double espresso mixed through would work or use
plain vanilla)

(If not used immediately any left over meringue
can be frozen. Put into a plastic piping bag and
freeze when cool.)

Method

For the Coffee Brûlée

Preheat oven to 140°C/120°C fan oven/gas 1
Put the cream and 180g of the sugar in a
saucepan and heat gently to dissolve the sugar.
Bring to the boil then remove from the heat.

Next, gently whisk together the egg yolks, sugar
and espresso and slowly add to the hot cream
mixture.

Using an ovenproof teacup or ramekin fill to ⅓
full with the mixture. Cook in the preheated oven
for 20–30 minutes until set. Leave to cool and
refrigerate.

For the Italian Meringue

Place the water and sugar in a saucepan with a
sugar thermometer, bring to the boil and simmer.

When the sugar temperature reaches 110°C
place the egg whites in a mixer and whisk until thick.

When the sugar syrup reaches 120°C add it to
the thick egg whites in a slow continuous stream
and whisk until glossy.

Place the meringue in a piping bag with a star
nozzle attached.

To Serve

Take the cups with the set coffee brûlée out of
fridge, add a layer of finely crumbled Amaretti
biscuits, then add a layer of coffee ice cream.
Next, pipe the Italian meringue in a spiral on top.

Using a blowtorch crisp the meringue to
a light brown colour or place in a hot oven or
3–4 minutes until light brown.

Serve on a saucer and serve with an Amaretti
biscuit on the side.

The Forge

Santon, Isle of Man, IM4 1JE
01624 610031
www.theforge.im

The Forge was born early in the spring of 2013, the spring of the snow! Just a few days after acquiring the keys in March, a hefty amount of snow hit the Isle of Man and for a few weeks the only way new owners Artan and Sarah Xhumrri, and their children, could visit the site was to park some way off and slip-slide down to the dilapidated gateway at the front of the building. This enforced closure allowed us time to really look at what we had invested in, seeing for the first time the potential of the beautiful grounds and surroundings.

We knew this site deserved to become something special, something true to its roots as an old Manx farm, something authentic. We stripped the building back to the bones, and left it there; the interior has been restored using old fittings and fixtures from around the site. We were lucky to uncover some gems such as our slate mantles for above the fire places (discovered buried under the old front porch), old tools hidden in sheds, reclaimed timbers and wiring from the original site.

The Forge smokehouse and grill, with its crackling fires and large open-plan dining rooms, allows for leisurely family-style feasting in a totally unique and independent environment where quality and authenticity is at the heart of everything we do.

The offering at the Forge is simple. Grown from our Albanian and British market town roots, we make every dish fresh, local and from scratch on-site. Our menu has a spine of freshly prepared, classic grill dishes, complemented by Mediterranean influences: in other words, modern British cookery.

The food offering is based on marinating, slow cooking, grilling and smoking the best meat, fish and vegetables we get our hands on. Very little is done after that, we dress it with our secret seasoning, extra virgin olive oil and freshly chopped flat-leaf parsley – home-grown whenever possible! You taste the quality of our local meat and seafood as nature intended. We have a passion to support our fellow local farmers and producers, and work closely with several expert farmers to maintain a quality supply in our restaurant.

When it comes to drinking, we hope to allow our guests to explore. Our botanical, crafted cocktails and infusions are the perfect way to soak up the flavoursome food offering. We have an eclectic wine boutique showcasing some of the world's best known types and producers, and we also source our Own Label house wines to be perfectly balanced with the food we create.

Wherever possible we grow our own, with budding gardens of herbs, flowers, fruit and vegetables. Our ketchup, butter and condiments are also homemade and our shop, both in-house and online, allows our guests to take a little of the Forge home to enjoy. The root of the Forge hospitality is simply getting around the table together for the best of all things

Starter from The Forge

Scallops with hazelnut butter
serves 1

Ingredients

3 scallops per person (in shell)

Hazelnut Butter

453g butter
100g hazelnuts (roasted)
garlic (to taste)
1 lemon (juice and zest)

a pinch of black pepper
a pinch of rock salt

To Serve

parsley (freshly chopped)
lemon wedges

Method

For the Hazelnut Butter

Soften the butter and mix all of the ingredients together until well combined.

Roll the mixture in greaseproof paper to create a log, and chill until needed.

For the Scallops

Preheat oven to 250oC/220oC fan oven/gas 9

Sear the scallops in a hot pan and place in their shells. Top each scallop with a slice of hazelnut butter and cook in the hot oven for 5 minutes.

To Serve

Sprinkle with fresh chopped parsley and lemon wedges and you may want to have some finger bowls at the ready!

Main course from The Forge

Blue boy burger

serves 4

Ingredients

Mushrooms

800g of your favourite mushrooms
sprig of rosemary
1 garlic clove (finely chopped)
2 tbsp oil for frying
salt and pepper

Burgers

1kg best quality steak mince
½ tsp ground black pepper
1 tsp garlic powder
1 tsp smoked paprika
2 tsp onion powder
1 tsp heaped salt

Burger Sauce

2 tbsp mayonnaise
1 tbsp BBQ sauce
1 tsp English mustard
pinch of smoked paprika

Garnish

tomato (thinly sliced)
onion (thinly sliced)
lettuce
gherkins (sliced)
coleslaw

To Serve

burger buns (toasted)

Method

For the Mushrooms

Thinly slice the mushrooms. Heat the rosemary, garlic and oil in a pan and gently sauté the mushrooms until soft and juicy. Season to taste.

For the Burgers

Preheat oven to 220°C/200°C fan oven/gas 7
Mix all the ingredients, except the cheese, together thoroughly and form into 4 round burger patties.

Pan-fry the burgers, they will need around 4–6 minutes on either side depending on how thick you have made them and how you like your burger cooked. Place the burgers onto a baking tray, top them with the cooked mushrooms and sprinkle with blue cheese and grated Cheddar (as much as you like!) and bake in the hot oven for 5 minutes or until the cheese has melted.

For the Sauce

Mix the ingredients together well.

To Serve

Spread the burger sauce onto to your favourite toasted burger buns, top with thinly sliced tomato, onion and crisp lettuce. Place the topped burger on the bun, add a couple of slices of gherkin and place the lid on top. Serve with fresh coleslaw and all your favourite condiments.

Dessert from The Forge

Brownie

serves 6-8

Ingredients

250g dark chocolate
175g butter
2 eggs
3 egg yolks
275g sugar
110g plain flour
1 tsp instant coffee
1 tsp vanilla extract

To Serve

ice cream
cream (whipped)

Method

Preheat oven to 190°C/170°C fan oven/gas 5

Melt the chocolate and butter together in a microwave oven, being careful not to overheat. Stop and stir the mixture every 20 seconds or so to make sure the mixture doesn't burn.

Cream the eggs, yolks and sugar with an electric mixer until light and fluffy. Next, fold the chocolate mixture into the eggs and sugar.

Slowly add the flour, coffee and vanilla extract and mix until all combined.

Line a 20cm (8 inch) baking tray with greaseproof paper and place the brownie mix in to the tray.

Cook for 35 minutes.

To Serve

Serve with whipped cream or ice cream for a delicious dessert.

Leonardo's

Stanley House, Castletown, IM9 1LF
01624 827635
www.facebook.com/Leonardosrestaurantiom

If you are visiting Castletown, the ancient capital of the Island, you may notice an Italian restaurant opposite Castle Rushen. In the shadow of the castle you can get the best Italian food presided over by head chef, Angiolino. The other chefs that work in Leonardo's come from all over the Mediterranean including Italy, Morocco, Spain, Cyprus and Portugal – all giving their unique and special twist to their food. Nowhere else in the world would you find so much of the Mediterranean in the shadow of a medieval castle.

Ben Batoul, the proprietor of Leonardo's, has worked in the catering industry for a number of years. Born in Morocco to a Spanish mother and a Moroccan father, he was brought up in Brussels and trained there to be a chef. He has worked in various prestigious establishments all over the world including working in Paris, Bermuda, Brussels and working aboard Cunard's *Queen Elizabeth 2*.

During the construction of this fabulous restaurant, builders uncovered an old Renaissance period water well, which can be viewed when trying the Mediterranean inspired cuisine. While you are there you may notice that the staff are all dressed to impress, and their service reflects that!

Starter from Leonardo's

Classic bouillabaisse

serves 4

Ingredients

227g shrimps
1.4 ltr (6 cups) water
1 bay leaf
12 whole black peppercorns
1 orange (peel only)
3 tbsp extra virgin olive oil
1 small onion (diced)
1 leek (white part only, thinly sliced)
2 small fennel bulbs (thinly sliced, fronds reserved)
4 garlic cloves (minced)
4 tomatoes (skins and seeds removed and diced)
237ml (1 cup) dry white wine

1 tsp fresh thyme
1 tsp fresh marjoram
½ tsp saffron threads
½ tsp ground cayenne pepper
227g sockeye salmon (skin removed, cut into 2.5cm wide strips)
227g cod (cut into 2.5cm wide strips)
227g Bay mussels
227g Manila clams
½ tsp kosher salt

Method

Peel the shrimp, reserving the shrimp shells. Bring the water to a simmer and add the shrimp shells, bay leaf, peppercorns and orange peel to the pot and simmer gently for 15 minutes.

Meanwhile, heat the olive oil over a medium heat in a heavy-bottomed soup pan. Add the onion, leek and fennel bulb and a pinch of salt, and slowly sweat them until tender but not browned (about 20 minutes).

Add the garlic and sauté for a few more minutes until the garlic is tender and fragrant. Next add the tomato and the wine. Turn up the heat until the

wine begins to boil, and cook until the wine is reduced by about half.

Strain the shrimp and orange stock into the onion mixture. Add the thyme, marjoram, saffron and cayenne and simmer for 10 minutes.

Add the fish first. About 2 minutes later add the mussels and clams. About 2 minutes after that add the shrimp. Simmer until the shrimp is just cooked through: about 2 more minutes.

Remove from the heat and serve immediately, garnishing each place with some reserved fennel fronds.

Main course from Leonardo's
Tortellini with salmon and ricotta
serves 4

Ingredients

500g spinach and ricotta tortellini
2 tbsp olive oil
250g smoked salmon (sliced)
1 bunch spring onions (chopped)
250g ricotta
150ml vegetable stock
10 dill stems (coarsely chopped)

To Serve

dill
pink pepper berries

Method

Cook the tortellini in boiling salted water according to the directions on the packet.

Meanwhile, heat the oil in a frying pan and sauté the salmon for 4 minutes. Add the spring onions, stir in the ricotta and stock and simmer for about 3 minutes.

When the pasta is cooked drain and set aside. Stir the dill into the sauce.

To Serve

Arrange the pasta on a serving plate with the salmon sauce and garnish with dill. Season with the pink pepper berries.

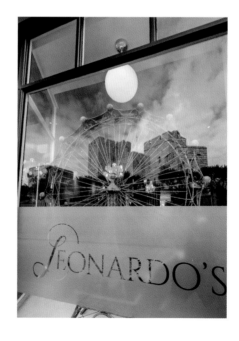

Pears poached in limoncello with crema di latte

serves 6

Ingredients

Crema di Latte

1 lemon
3 egg yolks
325g caster sugar
Pinch of ground cinnamon
40g flour
300ml milk
300ml single cream
6 firm pears (such as Williams or beurre bosc)
80ml limoncello

Method

For the Crema di Latte

Remove the lemon zest with a vegetable peeler, setting the lemon aside for later.

Place the egg yolks, 75g of the sugar, the cinnamon, flour, milk, cream and half the lemon zest into a saucepan. Whisk to combine, then cook over a low heat, stirring constantly, for 20 minutes or until slightly thickened. Pour the crema into a bowl, cover with buttered greaseproof paper and refrigerate until ready to serve.

For the Pears

Juice the lemon. Place the pears in a snug-fitting saucepan with enough water to cover. Add the remaining sugar, the lemon juice, the remaining zest and the limoncello and bring to the boil, stirring occasionally, to dissolve the sugar. Reduce the heat to low, cover and poach gently for 12 minutes or until cooked (this will depend on the ripeness of the pears). Remove the pears with a slotted spoon, and set aside.

Bring the pan of syrup to a rapid boil and reduce until thick enough to coat the back of a wooden spoon.

To Serve

Place a pear on each plate, drizzle with syrup and some crema di latte.

Chef's note: *Limoncello is an Italian-style lemon liqueur available from selected bottle shops.*

The Abbey

Rushen Abbey, Ballasalla, IM9 3DB
01624 822393
www.theabbeyrestaurant.co.im

Situated next to the ruins of an ancient monastery, The Abbey restaurant is steeped in history. Originally built with stones reclaimed from Rushen Abbey in the C18th, this fine country house has evolved over the years into the beautiful restaurant it is today.

The building, originally owned by Deemster Moore, was a fine private house until the 1830s when ownership transferred to Rev. W. Ward, a man who had designs of a more ecclesiastical nature for the property. His plan to build a 'splendid new church' fell through and in the 1840s the house became a boarding school for young ladies, run by sisters Miss Bell Anne and Ellen Stowell.

By 1866 the house was listed in trade directories as a new 'Country House Hotel' in Ballasalla, and by the turn of the C20th the hotel was a popular destination for visitors to the Island. The award-winning jam factory on site, run by Messrs Woods and Hardon, which operated from the late C19th through to the 1970s, brought a taste of the Isle of Man to the world, and must surely have furnished the jam for the strawberry cream teas enjoyed by visitors.

Today the Abbey Restaurant is a stylish, hidden gem set amid luscious green surroundings. Our large one hundred and forty cover dining room has a menu that changes daily, and which makes the best of the Island's seasonal produce, in the tradition of modern European cooking, with an accessible wine list predominantly sourced from France, Spain and Italy.

The Abbey is made up of four spaces which work together in perfect harmony: there are the two main restaurant areas, the garden room and the private dining room.

Children are welcome at The Abbey, with a children's menu, high chairs and junior chairs for your convenience and books and toys to keep your little ones entertained. An outside play area, which can be viewed from the garden room, is perfect for capturing your child's imagination while you dine in comfort.

Join us for a meal and discover relaxed, family friendly, fine dining at its best.

Starter from The Abbey
Home-smoked salmon and horseradish cream
serves 6

Ingredients

Salmon

180g salt
150g sugar
2 lemons (zest and juice)
2 tbsp dill (chopped)
500g freshest salmon (bones removed)

For Smoking

2 handfuls of smoking chips

Horseradish Cream

good quality horseradish sauce
double cream
salt and pepper

To Serve

lemon wedges
olive oil
freshly ground pepper

Method

For the Salmon

Mix the salt, sugar, lemon zest, lemon juice and dill together, and cover the fish in the mixture.

Chill in the fridge, in a plastic or glass container, for a minimum of 6 hours. Remove from the fridge, rinse well in cold water for 10 minutes then pat dry.

Burn the chips in a pan, allow them to smoulder and place the salmon, on top of a cake rack, above the smouldering wood chips.

Cover the pan tightly with tinfoil to seal in the smoke. Leave for 1 hour, then remove the fish and, when cooled, refrigerate well.

For the Horseradish Cream

Mix the horseradish sauce and cream together until well combined and season to taste.

To Serve

Slice as thinly as you can and serve with horseradish cream, lemon wedge, a drizzle of olive oil and freshly ground black pepper

Main course from The Abbey

Blackened beef fillet

smoked Cheddar dauphinoise, red wine and garlic purée, and watercress with garden greens

Ingredients

Blackened Beef Fillet

200g beef fillet per person
lots of salt, pepper and oil

Jus

2.3 ltr good beef stock (shop bought is fine)
If you'd like to home make your stock:
  6 large beef bones
  2 onions
  10 carrots
  2 tins of tinned tomatoes
  1 head of celery
  1 garlic bulb
  1 sprig sage
  1 sprig rosemary
  4 bay leaves
  100g tomato purée
  1 bottle red wine

6 shallots (chopped with skins)
beef trimmings

Smoked Cheddar Dauphinoise (serves 10)

20 large potatoes
400g smoked Cheddar cheese (grated)
150g butter
200ml double cream
300ml good chicken stock
1 sprig rosemary
salt and pepper to taste

Red Wine Garlic Purée (serves 10)

4 garlic bulbs (peeled and boiled)
275ml red wine
a pinch of salt

To Serve

watercress
your favourite green vegetables
butter

Method

For the Blackened Beef Fillet

Preheat oven to 60°C/gas ¼
Season the fillet well with salt and pepper.
Sear the beef all over, until very dark on all sides, in a very hot pan with a little oil.
Cook in the preheated oven for 1 hour.
Slice and serve.

For the Smoked Cheddar Dauphinoise

Preheat oven to 200°C/180°C fan oven/gas 6
Line an ovenproof dish with greaseproof paper.
Peel and very thinly slice the potatoes (use a mandolin for this if you can).
Cover the bottom of the dish with a couple of layers of the sliced potato, season with a little salt and pepper then add half of the cheese.
Cover this with another layer of potatoes and the rest of the cheese, then add the final layer of potatoes.
In a pan, melt the butter, cream, stock and rosemary together.
Pour the mixture over the potatoes and allow the liquid to sink into the dish.
Cover the dish with a layer of baking paper and then foil and bake in the oven for around 1 hour to 1½ hours until a knife easily slices though the potatoes.

For the Red Wine Garlic Purée

Place the boiled garlic in a pan with the wine and boil with a pinch of salt until the wine is reduced to almost nothing.
Blend in a food processor until smooth.
Add a little salt to taste.

For the Jus

To create the jus, first make the gravy.

If making your own stock first cover all of the stock ingredients with water, then boil in a large saucepan for 4 hours. Pass through a sieve. Further reduce the liquid down to 4 pints (roughly 2 litres).

To make the gravy, put the beef stock into a large pan, adding the red wine, shallots and any beef trimmings. Simmer gently for at least an hour to reduce to approx. 2 pints (1 litre) then add any roasting juices you may have.

Pass through a sieve.

To create the jus, reduce the gravy by simmering in a saucepan over a medium heat until it is reduced to 500ml.

To Serve

Warm your plates in the oven if possible.

Put a spoonful of garlic purée onto the dinner plate. Using the back of your spoon, smear the purée across the plate in a circle. Place a slice of the potatoes on top, followed by a slice of beef. Finish with a handful of watercress and a drizzle of jus. Serve with bowls of green vegetables in butter. or serve whole, allowing guests to help themselves.

Dessert from The Abbey

Trifle
serves 8

Ingredients

1 pack lady's finger biscuits
200g raspberries
150ml cream sherry
100ml raspberry coulis

1 ltr custard
1 ltr whipped cream
60g toasted almonds

Method

Place the lady's fingers in the base of a large glass serving bowl.

Sprinkle over the raspberries and douse in the sherry and the coulis.

Carefully cover in custard.

Top with the cream and the almonds.

Allow at least 4 hours in the fridge for the sponge fingers to absorb the sherry and coulis and go all mushy and boozy!

Eateries

It's no surprise that the Isle of Man is home to many superb, larger restaurants – the Island's reputation for excellent food shows no sign of slowing down. However, the rise in casual fine-dining is shown in the numerous eateries scattered around the Island.

Whether you prefer a quick bite to eat, a more informal, relaxed dinner option or a traditional high-tea, the eateries featured here are sure to delight your taste buds...

(from page 240)

Pantries

The wealth of natural resources on the Isle of Man, and the rise in demand for high-quality produce with low food miles, has led to the growth of small producers creating exceptional products for the Island's chefs and home cooks.

Artisan businesses serving the restauranteurs and Island's home kitchens create delicacies of quality rarely found elsewhere. The businesses featured in 'the pantry' will add a taste of the Isle of Man to your cooking.

(from page 278)

delicious recipes from THE ISLE of MAN **241**

Close Leece
Farm Shop and Café

Patrick Road, St Johns IM4 3BR
01624 307200
www.closeleecefarm.com

lose Leece farm has a reputation for producing high-quality award-winning foods. We raise our animals on pasture to the highest welfare standards and we believe that this produces the very best tasting foods. We are very proud to have been awarded 28 UK Great Taste Awards and British Charcuterie Awards, including a highly coveted 3 Star Great Taste Award for our chorizo.

In March 2019 we opened Close Leece Farm Shop and Café in a stunning, converted, former agricultural stone barn situated right in the heart of the farm, thereby creating a truly unique farm to fork experience. The shop features the full range of our own award-winning farm-produced meats,milk, cheese, eggs and honey, together with a wide range of Manx-made crafts, foods and drinks,including beers, ciders and gins, all selected by us to showcase the very best the Island has to offer

Seasonal and Manx are at the heart of the menu, which features meats from our own pasture-raised rare-breed Tamworth pigs and Loaghtan sheep or sourced from neighbouring farms, all complemented by Manx-

grown salads and vegetables. Seasonal fish dishes and locally smoked salmon also feature, together with a range of vegetarian options. The café specialty is the farm-produced charcuterie boards, which include a range of our salamis and chorizo handmade on the farm, including the unique Loaghtan lamb salami, together with our own Great Taste Award-winning goat's cheese.

Those with a sweet tooth are not ignored as home made scones, cakes and brownies made from our UK award-winning eggs, Isle of Man Creamery butter and Laxey flour are always on offer, along with a range of hot and cold desserts made from locally sourced ingredients.

The café area seats up to 80 over 2 floors and features a large woodburning stove for the winter months and floor-to-ceiling windows, through which you can watch the goats graze. Additional seating is available outside in the sheltered beer garden, which includes a children's swing together with chickens and goats to feed. Well-behaved dogs are welcome and even have their own menu featuring our special-recipe handmade dog friendly sausages!

Close Leece Farm Shop and Café

Chorizo and queenie linguine

serves 4

Ingredients

350g dry linguine
1 stick of Close Leece Farm chorizo
2 garlic cloves (finely chopped)
1–2 red chillies, to taste (finely chopped)
125ml Isle of Man Creamery double cream
1 bunch of parsley (freshly chopped)
350g Manx queenies
sea salt and freshly ground black pepper

To Serve

half a lemon

Method

Cook the linguine in salted water according to instructions or until the pasta is al dente, then drain and set aside.

Cube the chorizo and fry over a medium heat with the garlic and chillies for 2–3 minutes until the chorizo has released its oils. Remove the chorizo, garlic and chillies, leaving the oil in the pan, and set aside.

Pour the cream into a saucepan and heat over a medium to low heat, simmer until thickened and add the chopped parsley (reserving a little for the garnish), salt and pepper to taste.

In the same pan the chorizo was fried in, seal off the queenies over a high heat – don't overcook.

Remove from the heat and add the chorizo, garlic and chillies back to the queenies in the pan, then add the cooked linguine and enough cream to coat the pasta.

Mix together and serve with a chopped parsley garnish on top with a wedge of lemon

Wine Down

24 Duke St., Douglas, IM1 2AY
01624 624777   www.winedown.im

A chance conversation at the end of April 2018 led to a swift decision to set up a new concept for the Isle of Man.

The brainchild of Anne Harrison, with 30 years in the wine trade, and Roy Macfarlane, almost as many years in the kitchen, Wine Down opened its doors on August 6th 2018. We got together to share our passion for food and wine and to offer a unique dining experience on the Island.

The Team

From the outset, the aim has been to offer great quality food and wine in a relaxed environment. We see personal and friendly service as key to the business and pride ourselves on the quality of our hard-working team, both front and back of house. Our two talented young chefs, Graham and David, who joined us earlier this year, work hard to ensure Roy's high standards are consistently achieved and the nature of the menu gives them the opportunity to be creative. We have invested in new kitchen equipment, enabling them to keep coming up with new and exciting dishes. Gary, our kitchen assistant/chef, has been working with Roy for over 10 years and is the engine that keeps us all going, with both his work ethic and his incessant banter!

Front of house is Maggie, who joined us in our first month. She is the creative member of the team and she is responsible for putting together our bespoke gift packs.

When she arrived, the extent of her wine

knowledge was 'it's red or white', but now she can confidently advise on our range, and grape varieties such as Xinomavro, Thrapsathiri and Zweigelt roll off her Irish tongue! Desi is our newest member, coming to us from Theatre of Wine in London. Desi has worked in the wine trade for almost 20 years in places as far afield as California, China and her native Bulgaria. Her passion for wine is unsurpassable and her warm and friendly nature has made her very popular with our customers in the short time she has been on the Island.

The Wine Bar/Restaurant

Our menu is very flexible, allowing customers to enjoy a traditional three-course meal or to select several dishes to share. The size of the dishes varies and allows everyone to eat as much or as little as they wish.

Our wine list by the glass changes regularly and we have a selection of over 200 wines available by the bottle. Our licence allows customers to take away part bottles so if you wish to order a bottle but only want to drink a glass, we can cork it for you to take home and enjoy later.

The Shop

Unbeknown to many, we are also a shop and are immensely proud of our range of wines, which is ever changing. We have been delighted with the response so far to the quality and breadth of our selection. We offer discounts on case sales of 6 and 12 bottles and deliver across the Island in our own van. Our opening hours for the shop are 10am until 10pm and it is possible to park outside the front door after 5pm in the evening.

You are very welcome to call in at any time to browse the shelves and maybe enjoy a coffee or a glass of wine! There is always someone here to give friendly expert advice and we have at least 12 bottles open to taste, including a premium one, so you can try before you buy. If you do not have time to come in or prefer to shop on-line, you can visit our website www.winedown.im

The Masterclasses, Tastings and Food Pairings

We run regular Masterclasses and have covered subjects such as Greek wines, Sauvignon Blanc and sparkling wines. These are tutored tastings accompanied by light bites to complement each wine. If you are interested in learning more about wine in a friendly, informal and relaxed atmosphere, sign up to our mailing list by going to our website and completing our form.

We hold twice-yearly tastings at which you can taste around 30 wines with light bites. We find our customers get settled in for the afternoon and enjoy a meal afterwards. An ideal opportunity to meet people, make new friends and simply relax.

The School

Anne and Desi are undeniably the two most experienced wine specialists on the Island, qualified to Level 4 and 3 respectively of the Wine and Spirit Education Trust (WSET) Examinations. Anne has recently qualified further, passing the rigorous Educator course and is the local Approved Programme Provider, enabling her to teach to Level 3 on the Island. The WSET qualifications are recognised throughout the world, and in association with WSET in the North West, Anne and Desi will offer WSET qualifications in the near future. If you have an interest in, or work with wine, and wish to study for a formal qualification, please get in touch at relax@winedown.im The course will be educational, yet relaxed, and will take place in Wine Down with the examination in the approved venue of Ballakermeen High School.

We love to celebrate here at Wine Down and we find every opportunity we can! If there is a National or International Day for a grape variety, you can rest assured we will put on a selection of wines with a tasting menu to match. In September we are celebrating Grenache Day and in November it is the turn of Merlot, Tempranillo and Zinfandel.

In addition, we have a food and wine pairing every few days so there is always something new to try at Wine Down.

If you have not yet signed up to our mailing list, why not call in to see us, call us on 624777 or drop us an email at relax@winedown.im

We look forward to welcoming you to the relaxing experience of Wine Down.

Charcuterie and Artisan Cheese board with crispy bread and fruits

To create an enticing charcuterie and cheese board that will delight your guests, be sure to use a balance of mild, sharp, creamy, crumbly and blue cheeses and the finest meats available to you.

Arrange the meat and cheese on a large decorative board, along with a selection of grapes, apples (sliced to your preference) and artisan crispy breads.

You may use whatever you wish according to your taste and budget (a small, select choice can be just as exciting as a larger offering). As an example we include: chorizo, nduja, salami, Cashel blue, Manx vintage Cheddar, Brie de Meaux and Red Leicester

Wine Pairing

Austrian Plum St Laurent

The St Laurent grape is named after St Lawrence's Day, August 10th, the date that this grape variety ripens. It is indigenous to Austria and is becoming more widely planted and recognised for its fine quality.

Some say it is Austria's answer to Syrah, yet with the finesse and elegance of Pinot Noir. Some believe that it is actually a cross between Pinot Noir and an unknown variety.

This delicately aromatic, smooth and medium-bodied, yet full-flavoured, wine comes from the Pfaffl estate. It has aromas of cherry and coffee, leading to flavours of strawberry, plum and cherry and a long, smooth finish.

Medium in body, with gentle tannins, it could also be served lightly chilled. Whether served chilled or at room temperature, it makes a great partner to our charcuterie and cheese selection.

Aaron House

Aaron House, The Promenade, Port St Mary, Isle of Man, IM9 5DE
01624 835702   www.aaronhouse.co.uk

Aaron House is a 5-star guest house overlooking the beautiful Chapel Bay of Port St Mary. Apart from their beautifully decorated and truly authentic guest rooms, Aaron House is renowned for their indulgent afternoon teas. All of their afternoon teas reflect the very best of local, Manx produce and are prepared daily by a team who are passionately dedicated to their craft. The team at Aaron House have spent many years perfecting this quintessentially English tradition and have blended it with their head baker's outstanding knowledge of Swiss pastries and confectionery. These outstanding afternoon teas are all presented with a glamorous sense of tradition and occasion and are served in an atmospheric Victorian dining room. They feature a tantalising selection of finger sandwiches, tempting handcrafted savouries and an assortment of the finest patisseries, scones and fresh chocolates. They are also served with a delightful variety of premium teas and coffee. Enjoying an afternoon tea at Aaron House is a splendid way to pass an afternoon. Their tea room is also fully licensed.

To reserve a table please telephone 01624 835702. Please note that only advanced pre-bookings are accepted. No walk-in service is provided.

Aaron House
Manx ale fruit loaf
serves 4

This loaf will last up to four weeks, so we make two. Bushy's Premium Ale works well. Delicious on its own or buttered and served with a hunk of Manx Vintage Cheddar.

Ingredients

500ml Bushy's Premium Ale
85g IOM Creamery whey butter or butter
170g soft dark brown sugar
600g good quality mixed vine fruits
140g orange peel
170g Laxey Mills self-raising flour (sieved)
170g Laxey Mills wholemeal or rye flour (sieved)
1 level tsp bicarbonate of soda
1 tsp mixed spice
3 free-range eggs

Method

Put the ale, butter, sugar, fruit and peel into a saucepan and heat gently until hot. Remove from the heat, cover and leave overnight.

Preheat oven to 140–150°C/gas 2

Add the sieved flours, bicarbonate of soda, spice and eggs to the fruit mixture and mix well. Divide into 2 loaf tins lined with parchment paper.

Bake for approximately 1¼ hours until risen, pale brown and firm to the touch.

Leave in the tin until cool.

Decorate as you like or leave it plain.

Store in a cool dry place.

The Dovecote Tearoom

Main Road Kirk Michael, IM6 1AB
01624 878534

The Dovecote Tearoom is a shabby chic gem hidden in Kirk Michael.

It started out as a tearoom and gift shop, however, the tearoom proved very popular so we expanded into the gift shop area to provide a relaxed, friendly atmosphere.

We pride ourselves on serving good home-cooked food and baking all cakes, scones, meringues, puddings, soups and main courses on the premises using quality Manx ingredients where possible.

The recipe over the page is one of our best-selling cakes!

The Dovecote Tearoom
Cherry and marzipan cake

Ingredients

200g butter
(softened, plus a little extra for the tin)
200g caster sugar
4 free-range eggs
200g self-raising flour
200g glacé cherries (chopped)

100g ground almonds
2–3 drops almond extract
250g marzipan
50g blanched almonds
icing sugar for dusting

Method

Preheat the oven to 160°C/140°C fan oven/gas 3

Butter and line a deep 20cm round cake tin.

Beat the butter and sugar in a bowl until light and creamy then pour in the eggs, a little at a time, and beat well after each addition. Next, mix in the flour then fold in the cherries, ground almonds and almond extract until well mixed.

Spoon half the mixture into the tin.

Roll out the marzipan to a 19cm circle, lay it on top of the mixture in the tin, then cover with the rest of the mixture, level, and scatter blanched almonds on top.

Bake for 90 minutes (check after an hour) until a skewer inserted comes out clean.

Leave to cool in the tin for 20 minutes before turning out on to a wire rack and cooling completely. Dust with icing sugar before serving.

Secret Pizza

Barracks Square Castletown, IM9 1NR
01624 822833 www.thesecretpizzaco.im

From modest beginnings in 2016, the Secret Pizza Co. has moved on from Tom and Kylie touring the Island in their Diahatsu Hijet, Paolo, to permanent premises in Barracks Square, Castletown.

After kitting Paolo out with a 600kg clay oven (a bit different to his former life as a florist's delivery van) they served their pizza throughout the Island, visiting events and testing the market.

When their following became so large that they outgrew their preparation kitchen in Port St Mary, Tom and Kylie knew that the time was right to settle into premises, and now their customers can visit them for the finest artisan pizzas.

The menu is small, but mighty, being tailored to the week's weather and the best seasonal, local produce available. All the pizzas are 12 inch (ish), hand stretched and start off vegetarian, topped with freshly prepared ingredients to order, but if you fancy adding a little extra to your pizza, loaded wedges or mac and cheese, the company has teamed up with their friends over at Cow & Pig Smokehouse for a bit of smoky BBQ action.

The Secret Pizza Co. aims to make everyone a happy pizza eater, with vegan cheese available to make any of the recipes vegan friendly too!

Secret Pizza
The Big Cheese
makes two 10 inch (ish) pizzas

The Big Cheese aims to celebrate the epic flavours of Isle of Man Creamery Cheddars, atop a beautiful, light, all Manx dough!

Ingredients

Dough

500g Laxey Queen flour
1 tsp salt
1 tsp fresh yeast or ¼ tsp instant yeast
325ml lukewarm water

Toppings

1 tin of good quality plum tomatoes
5 or 6 fresh basil leaves
Isle of Man Creamery mild, coloured Cheddar (grated)
Isle of Man Creamery mature Cheddar (grated)

Toppings (continued)

Parmesan cheese (grated)
mozzarella (grated)
pinch of dried oregano
Laxey Mills semolina
pinch of salt

Pesto

Isle of Man Creamery Vintage Cheddar
walnuts

Method

For the Dough

In a large bowl, place the flour and salt together. In another bowl, rub the yeast between your fingers in the water to dissolve it (if using instant yeast add this to the flour as instructed on the packet). Add the yeast and water mixture slowly to the flour and mix well with your hands until the dough starts to come together.

Shape the dough into a ball and leave to rest, covered with a damp tea towel for 10 minutes. After this time, you will find the dough much easier to work with.

Knead the dough for 5 minutes and split into two. Knead each piece for a couple of minutes each and form into balls. Sprinkle some flour on a tea towel and place the dough on it, cover with another slightly damp tea towel. Leave to rise in a warm place for 1 hour.

Prepare the Toppings

Drain a little of the liquid off the tomatoes, put the remaining tomatoes, basil and salt in a bowl and crush the tomatoes in your hands – leaving some juicy bits in the sauce!

Combine the mild, coloured Cheddar and mature Cheddar in a bowl and make sure they are mixed up well

Place all pesto ingredients into a blender and blend until smooth.

Pesto (continued)

50g basil
1 garlic clove
30g olive oil
½ tsp salt
½ tsp black pepper

During the wild garlic season (March to the beginning of June) try replacing the basil and garlic with some wild garlic leaves for a beautiful, peppery, even Manxer pesto!

Once the Dough has Risen

Preheat oven to 250°C/230°C/gas 9

Sprinkle some flour onto a clean work surface and with your fingers spread the dough into a roughly round shape, making sure to push all the air out to the edge to form a crust. Make the dough as thin as a pancake, but be careful not to split the dough. Sprinkle some Laxey Mills semolina on two large, flat baking trays and place the pizza bases on them.

Spread 2 tablespoons of the tomato mixture onto the bases, leaving about a 2cm space around the edge. Sprinkle with a pinch of grated Parmesan. Take a generous handful of the Cheddar mix and sprinkle over the tomato. Then take a generous handful of grated mozzarella and spread over the cheddars. Finally sprinkle a pinch of dried oregano over the pizza.

Bake for in the oven for about 7 minutes ... a couple minutes more if you like your pizza crispy.

Once baked, slide the pizzas onto a board, drizzle with pesto and leave to stand for around one minute before serving on plates.

Chef's note: *this dough recipe is an adaptation of our restaurant dough, designed to be quick and convenient for those last-minute pizza nights!*

Ticket Hall

Douglas Railway Station, Bank Hill, Douglas IM1 4LL
01624 627888   www.ticket-hall.com

After a major refurbishment the Tickethall re-opened its doors on 11th March 2017. Trish Hoy, who had worked there for seven years, took over the reins from her partner Steve Quirk. Our main team have over 100 years' experience in the catering trade and have all been working together for five years now.

The main restaurant is now upstairs, and to furnish this we scoured antique shops, and had seats recovered in the material used for the dining car, bringing the railway into the theme and blending old furniture into a new building. We kept

on our famous Fireman's Breakfast, served on a shovel, which comes from the tradition of the railway workers who would take their raw ingredients, put them on a shovel, and cook their breakfast on the fire.

Breakfast is served daily from 8–11 a.m and lunch is served from 12–2.30 p.m. Our coffee shop is on the ground floor, serving a selection of homemade cakes and sandwiches.

As if this is not enough, we also do the catering for the dining car, which has become a huge success.

Ticket Hall

Pan-seared locally caught fillet of hake

on a bed of cheesy leeks

serves 4

Ingredients

½ onion (finely diced)
1 bay Leaf
½ glass of white wine
120ml fish stock
(or using 1 fish stock cube)
500g Bryan Radcliffe's leeks
(washed and chopped)
240ml Isle of Man Creamery
double cream
4 x 150–200g locally
caught hake fillets
200g Isle of Man Creamery
Manx Mature Cheddar (grated)
a drizzle of olive oil
2 knobs of butter
salt and pepper

Method

Place a knob of butter in a saucepan and heat until just beginning to foam then add the diced onion and bay leaf. Cook until the onions turn translucent.

Next add the white wine and fish stock then reduce by two-thirds. Add the leeks and cream then cook until the cream has reduced to a rich sauce and the leeks are cooked. Put to one side.

In a non-stick pan, heat some oil until smoking. Season the hake and place in the hot pan skin-side down and leave until the skin is golden brown.

Turn the hake over, add another knob of butter and take the pan off the heat.

Reheat the leeks, add the grated cheese and stir until the cheese has melted.

To Serve

Place the cheesy leeks on the plate first, laying the hake on top.

Garnish and serve.

The Shed

Far end of the promenade, Laxey, IM4 7DD
01624 863151

Opened in 2017, The Shed has provided the Isle of Man with a new, quirky concept for outdoor eating, no matter what the weather. With uninterrupted views of the gorgeous Laxey Bay, in an area of the promenade sheltered by the stunning cliff side, you can be guaranteed of a very warm and friendly welcome and exceptional service from Team Shed.

Inspired by a lifelong love of the beach, whether relaxing on the golden sands on a glorious day or being wrapped up watching the crashing waves on a brisk winter's day, owners Bev and Richard Clegg were frustrated at the lack of beachside eateries where you could enjoy our beautiful beaches all year round. So, with cosy blankets, patio heaters, hot water bottles and some quaint bunting thrown in, The Shed was born.

Our philosophy is to 'keep it local' and we are proud that 95% of our food, drink and gift suppliers are just that, and are exceptionally good too. We have a simple all-day menu with the focus on keeping it fresh and doing it well. Freshly made paninis, using delicious mature Cheddar cheese from the Isle of Man Creamery, locally made Pork and Black Pudding Pie served with mushy peas,

homemade cakes and fresh barista coffee are just a few items on our menu. If you're looking for something a little healthy, our raw, natural cold-pressed vegetable and fruit juices, made by our sister company in Laxey, Creative Juices, will fit the bill. Always a popular choice for our customers, who we fondly refer to as 'shedders', other homemade delights such as energy balls, lemon sorbet, and juicy ice lollies make a great choice too.

Enjoy a very special experience, a one-of-a-kind on the Isle of Man, whether it's fresh food to grab and go, a relaxing lunch with family and friends on the beach snuggled on a bean bag, or coffee and cake under our shelter watching the world go by, there's something for everyone at The Shed, even our four-legged friends have their own 'Doggy Station'.

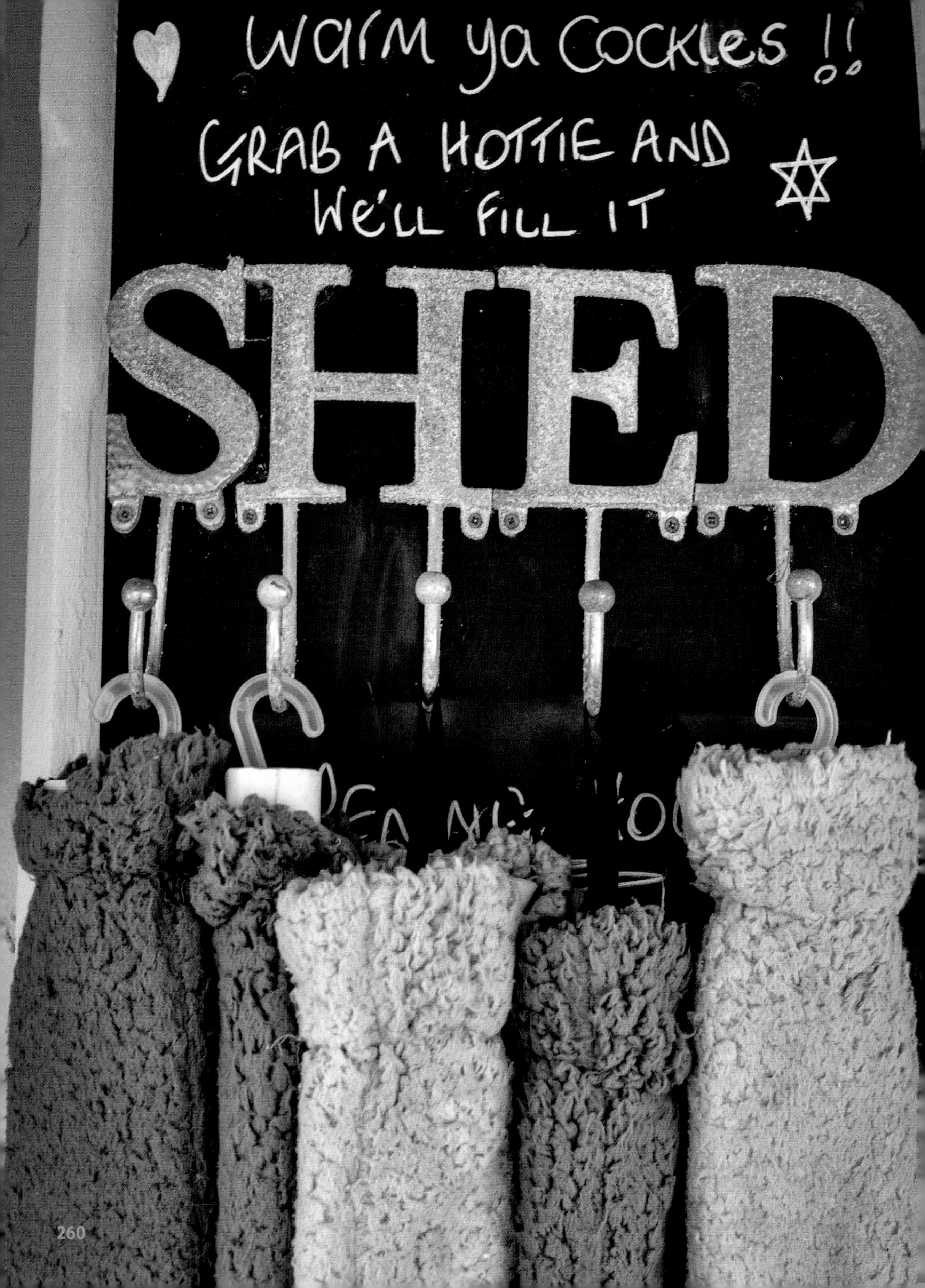
warm ya Cockles !!
GRAB A HOTTIE AND
WE'LL FILL IT
SHED

The Shed

The zest factor!

serves 1

Juicing is basically a quick way to get loads of nutrients into your body at once. Hooray for health! Besides being delicious, this juice is also incredibly healthy with Vitamins A, K, beta carotene from the carrots, Vitamin C and polyphenols from the apples and antioxidants and folate from the beetroot. Beetroot is such a great blood-builder.

Ingredients

½ bulb Manx beetroot
4 medium Manx carrots
⅓ lemon (unwaxed)
2 Manx apples

Method

Using a centrifugal or cold-press juicer.

There is no need to peel the ingredients (apart from the woody skin around the ends of the beetroot which can make it taste a little too earthy). Simply scrub the vegetables and fruit well and chop into chunky pieces. Feed through your juicer, starting and finishing with an apple, and bingo ... 500ml of healthy, nutritious goodness in a glass.

Without a centrifugal or cold-press juicer.

If you don't have a juicer, it doesn't mean you can't enjoy this super-tasty juice. Simply pop everything in a blender and whizz until pulp. Then press it through a fine mesh strainer until all of the juice is out. This may sound like a bit of work but it's really quite simple. Discard the pulp and enjoy your juicy juice.Why not use the pulp in a creative way – make doggy biscuits, use it in cakes or pop it on your compost heap in the garden. No waste!

What the Fork

WTF.co.im 07624 315284

While most street food businesses start life outside, then move indoors, never ones for the conventional, head chefs and owners, Gareth and Richard, decided to do the opposite.

Starting life in 2015 as What The Fork Café in Douglas, the business soon gained a five-star reputation on Facebook and Trip Advisor and was popular with locals and visitors alike.

Based around the principle of using local produce to create global cuisine, What The Fork were early innovators of modern, unique and exciting street food on the Island. The success and reputation of the café led to the purchase of a market stall, from which we first traded, then a trailer and finally our 1985 custom Mercedes street food truck (road tax of £19 a year).

2019 has been a very busy year for WTF, where we have catered for weddings, birthdays, major company opening events and Bushy's TT Village. Bushy's is a particular favourite, as it allows us to work hard and play hard (bit too hard sometimes, but all work and no play ...). Oh, and listen to some great bands too.

What The Fork have also branched out into many new areas, bringing the quality and innovation we are known for to peoples work places.

We now provide Canteen services to one of the worlds largest Egaming companies. Information about our range of services can be found at our website WTF.CO.IM

From the start, we have always tried to involve our cultural influences in our menus, from Film, Hip hop, Indie music and Street art . Which is why you will find such dishes as The Naan Inch Nails, our curry, The Caje Against The Machine, a spicy chicken Queasadilla and The Notorious P.I.G., our Manx Pulled Pork Taco on the menu.

Opposite is the recipe for another of our dishes, The Cypress Grill. We have simplified it slightly, as not everyone owns their own Smokehouse and these ingredients can be found in any supermarket.

What the Fork
The Cypress grill

Ingredients

Pulled Beef Brisket

1kg finest Manx brisket
1 beef stock cube
1 chicken stock cube
2 tsp mixed herbs

2 tsp smoked paprika (pimenton)
2 tsp Cajun seasoning
2 bay leaves
oil for frying
salt and pepper

To Serve

tortillas
ciabatta
slaw
Manx Cheddar
chorizo

Method

Preheat oven to 160°C/gas 3 or use a pressure cooker.

Cut the brisket into chunks the size of a block of butter. This will give you the long strands of beef which are essential to the recipe. Shallow fry your beef to get some colour on it.

The quick and slow methods:

For speed, place all the ingredients in a pressure cooker. Add enough water to nearly cover the meat. If you don't have a pressure cooker, put the ingredients in a deepish baking tray. Add enough water to nearly cover the meat. Cover the baking tray. The pressure cooker method takes around 2.5 hours from when it starts whistling.

The oven method, at 160°C will take closer to 8 hours. Well worth the wait, but a 7-litre pressure cooker is around £25 and a solid investment.

When the brisket is cooked, you should be able to break it up with two forks. If you can't, cook it for a bit longer. Pour off the liquor into a jug and save. Pull the beef apart into strands, then add the liquor slowly. You are after a moist mix, which is shiny, but not wet.

To Serve

Serve on tortillas or on ciabatta with slaw and melted Manx Cheddar. It's great with some chorizo as well. Now, open a cold one of your choice and chill.

Versa:
a pop-up restaurant concept

Shore oad, Port Erin
inforversa@gmail.com   Instagram.com/versaiom

Versa is a new restaurant concept that brings a fresh take on our definition of 'local produce'. Focusing on foraged ingredients and produce available within walking distance of the establishment, chef and owner Pippa Lovell aims to reinvent the dining scene on the Isle of Man through her weekly, changing, evening servings. Bigger than starter size, but less than a main, these servings showcase the produce that is 'at its best in that moment and in that place'.

Versa offers a vegan, fish, vegetarian, meat and sweet option in the evenings. During the daytime, Versa offers a monthly, changing, snack menu consisting of wild produce 'bar-snack style' featuring puffball mushroom arancini with a Port St Mary nasturtium aioli, and fried pork with beef mayo and foraged kimchi, to name a few.

'After recently relocating to the Isle of Man, I immediately fell in love with the landscape and the foraging opportunities available,' says Pippa. 'I love the sense of real community and support that the people offer, so I decided to open up restaurant "Versa" in a space already so profound, a place where my business could co-exist in an environment where people held similar values. This just happened to be an upcycled coal shed producing foraged wines. Versa offers wine pairings with each and every dish, as I try to make full use of this exciting collaboration.'

Pippa is heavily influenced by her time cooking in Scandinavia and after seeing how environmentally friendly and authentic the dining scene is there, she believes the Isle of Man has incredible potential to follow in its footsteps. Pippa feels that the Island can become a 'foodie destination' whilst simultaneously using the restaurant business as a catalyst for climate change initiatives and biodiversity.

'If we love something we will want to preserve it'

The ethics behind Versa are just this. Pippa believes that the key to preserving the industry is through loving what we do in our day-to-day, but also loving the ingredients we are using and being proud of them. Using hyper-local ingredients reduces carbon emissions and packaging, and also keeps the integrity of the ingredients, so that nutrition and taste isn't tainted. Why use watercress that has travelled hundreds of miles through a several-step process when it grows in abundance in the wild on our doorstep?

The menu is designed so that people can share and talk about the food, but you are also welcome to have the whole menu as a tasting menu with wine pairings. Booking is recommended Friday and Saturday and look out for ticketed events such as foraging tours, lunch and wine flights around Port Erin Bay.

Versa

Wild puffball mushroom, barley, preserved wild garlic and foraged herbs

serves 4

This recipe involves very little cooking. The idea is to marry flavours on a plate and keep the integrity of the ingredients

Ingredients

100g pearl barley
1 ltr vegetable stock using Manx vegetables only
100g pickled wild garlic leaves (picked in May)
250ml Ellerslie oil
4 local egg yolks
100g wild puffball mushroom (chopped)
50g Manx butter
2g wild thyme or Staarvey Farm thyme
salt and pepper

To Serve

hairy bittercress
(from Silverdale Glen in August)
yarrow flowers
(from Langness in August)

Method

Firstly, put the barley and vegetable stock in a pan and simmer until all of the stock has disappeared and the barley is chewy but not hard. Season to taste.

Meanwhile, blitz the wild garlic and the Ellerslie oil in a blender for ten minutes. Pass the oil through a sieve and a J-cloth.

Blitz the egg yolks and a little salt in a blender and very slowly add the garlic oil you have just made. This will gradually thicken to a mayonnaise consistency.

Quickly sauté the mushrooms in the Manx butter on a high heat with the thyme for 20 seconds. They must be golden brown and firm.

To Serve

Arrange the ingredients on a plate with the foraged herbs.

Tea Junction

14 Castle Street, Douglas, IM1 2EU

01624 616578   tea@theteajunction.im   www.theteajunction.im   www.shop.theteajunction.im

A warm welcome and a friendly face await you at The Tea Junction. Situated in Castle Street, Douglas, we've created a space where you can relax and enjoy life, one sip at a time. The Isle of Man's first true tea shop, we offer you the opportunity to sample and purchase nearly thirty varieties of loose-leaf tea and infusions of the highest grade. Our teas are sourced from suppliers who trade ethically with small companies and estates guaranteeing the freshest and highest quality teas available.

The Tea Junction, a concept unique to the Island opened its door in May 2015 and doubled in capacity after the first six months. As a nation, Britain consumes 70 million cups of coffee per day, but 165 million cups of tea are consumed in comparison! These days the nation is seeking an experience in tea, not just a tea bag in a pot. All our teas are loose leaf and brewed with precision at the correct temperature and for the correct amount of time. A real success story at the quieter end of town, this busy little tea shop is so much more.

An array of tasty breakfasts and lunches, from salads, paninis, quiches, jacket potatoes, soups and sandwiches, everything homemade and handcrafted for maximum enjoyment. If gin is your thing, we've got a range of 12 different fruity and tea-infused gins to be found nowhere else. Everything is available to enjoy in the café or take home with you, including all of our loose-leaf teas in handy re-sealable bags.

You can purchase all our teas, gins and tea accessories online too. Gift vouchers are available to purchase online or in-store.

Our Afternoon Tea is reputed to be one of the best on the Island and we can even serve Afternoon Tea with bubbles or G&Tea. Our hot chocolate is made with the finest Belgian chocolate, rich and decadent. In addition to tea we also make a great cup of coffee and we have a host of other homemade treats to delight and stimulate your taste buds.

The real stars of the show are our staff, and because of them we have won awards in customer service. Our international team of creatives in the kitchen are Angel from Mallorca and Michelle from Malta. Michelle has been with us from the start of our journey. Between them they have fashioned some amazing and indulgent creations both sweet and savoury. The cakes are a reflection of the fanatical way in which these guys work their magic.

We promise an intimate and relaxed experience that offers something different and ensures you enjoy a memorable experience every time.

Tea Junction
Honey cloud catcher cake

Ingredients

Cloud Catcher Tea Sponge

250ml Manx milk
3 tbsp of Tea Junction Cloud Catcher tea
480g caster sugar
6 large white eggs
1 tsp vanilla extract
300g Laxey Glen Mills Flavo plain flour
1.5 tsp baking powder
110ml vegetable oil
30g Manx honey

Buttercream Frosting

3 large white eggs
200g caster sugar
120g water
600g Manx soft butter
(room temperature, cut into small cubes)
4 tsp vanilla extract

To Serve

½ jar Tea Junction Cloud Catcher jam
Manx fresh berries (seasonal)

Continued on page 266

Honey cloud catcher cake

Method

Preheat oven to 150°C/130°C fan oven/gas 2 Spray 3 cake pans with non-stick spray and then line the bottoms with circles of parchment paper. Set aside.

Heat up the milk with the tea and leave to steep until cool, you should get 200ml out of this. Pass through a sieve and set aside.

Beat the sugar, eggs and vanilla extract. Then sift the flour and baking powder and fold into the egg mix. Slowly add the oil and the milky tea. Whisk with a hand whisk until well combined, but be careful not to overmix, just mix until large lumps are gone, small lumps are fine. Divide the batter evenly between the prepared cake tins.

Place into the oven to bake for 45 minutes or until a toothpick inserted into the centre of one of the cakes comes out clean.

When cooked, drizzle the cake with Manx honey and transfer to a wire cooling rack to cool completely before frosting.

For the Buttercream Frosting

Beat the egg whites, slowly add in 120g of the sugar and continue beating until soft peaks form.

In a medium saucepan add the remaining sugar and water, then place on a medium to low heat. Stir until the sugar melts and becomes clear. Maintain at a medium to high heat until the temperature reads 112–115°C/235–240°F on a sugar thermometer. Immediately, drizzle the sugar into the mixer containing the egg whites and run the mixer until the meringue is cool/tepid.

Switch to a paddle attachment, and add the room temperature butter into the running mixer one tablespoon piece at a time. Add the vanilla extract. Beat until the butter is combined and the mixture has reached a silky consistency.

To Assemble the Cake

Place the first layer of cake on your cake stand or plate.

Chef's note: *the cake layers shouldn't have a rounded dome on top of them, but if they do, cut them off before stacking.*

Add frosting and jam and spread into an even layer. Add the second layer of cake and another layer of frosting and jam. Top the cake with the remaining layer. Use the rest of the frosting to ice the outside of the cake and smooth it evenly.

Decorate with fresh Manx berries.

Foraging Vintners

13 Shore Rd, Port Erin, Isle of Man IM9 6LN
www.foragingvintners.com

Foraging Vintners is a seaside winery that specialises in non-grape-based sparkling wines, ciders and ginger beer. They are best known for their Rhubarb Fizz, which is a rhubarb sparkling wine that is available on draught taps at the Winery Bar in Port Erin.

The winery is located on the quayside of Port Erin and celebrates all of the wonderful produce that the British Isles offer. The products are all made on the premises, including their premium line of méthode traditionnelle sparkling wines, similar to Champagne style wines, that are not made with any grapes. This premium range of bottle products includes:

· Rhunessa Méthode Traditionnelle Rhubarb Sparkling Wine 12.8%ABV 75cl

· Eltoora Méthode Traditionnelle Elderflower Sparkling Wine 12.8%ABV 75cl

· Mildoona Méthode Traditionnelle Honey Sparkling Wine 12.8%ABV 75cl

· Benvarrey Méthode Traditionnelle Apple Sparkling Wine 12.8%ABV 75cl

The winery is one of the few in the world to focus on non-grape méthode traditionnelle sparkling wines in this volume. These sparkling wines are suitable to drink on their own or mixed in a cocktail.

Opposite you will find one of our cocktail recipes that is a favourites of the clientele at Foraging Vintners.

Foraging Vintners also make sparkling wines (that are in kegs), ciders and ginger beer at their seaside winery. These kegged products include:

· Rhubarb Fizz 12.0%ABV

· Elderflower Fizz 12.0%ABV

· Honey Fizz 12.0%ABV

· Apple Fizz 12.0%ABV

· Longtail Apple Cider 5.0%ABV

· Longtail Rhubarb Cider 5.0%ABV

· Longtail Honey Cider 5.0%ABV

· Longtail Ginger Beer 5.0%ABV

Mary Beth and Ian both relocated to the Isle of Man eight years ago and their business 'popped' from their hobby booze production in their garden shed. Their neighbours and friends affectionately named their garden shed the 'Little Wooden Pub'.

Due to its popularity the couple recognised a demand for tap wines, ciders and cocktails, and three years ago they took the leap and up-cycled an old coal shed located near the breakwater of Port Erin Bay into a winery and bar.

They work with local farmers who are committed to using ecological methods to produce the raw ingredients or source them from the British Isles. They have even taken several tonnes of seaweed from the local beach and tilled it into the soil to prepare the grounds for the rhubarb field otherwise known as the 'Rhub-yard'.

There have been some teething problems that come with being one of the few winemakers to specialise in non-grape wines at this level. They quickly learned that they have become the experts, as most consultants strictly base their knowledge on the grape production.

This has created a steep learning curve for the former lawyer and oil rig electrician, but together they can see the promise in what they have created.

Their belief is simple. Use the produce that thrives and is local, and find the alchemy that creates something truly unique and beautiful. Also, enthusiasm gets you everywhere and a bit of fizz and pop helps too!

Foraging Vintners

Rhugo

Our rhubarb version of the classic Hugo Champagne Cocktail.

serves 1

Ingredients

25ml mix Freshly Foraged Elderflower Syrup and Dry Gin
25ml Dry Gin (optional)
150ml Rhunessa Rhubarb Sparkling Wine
ice

To Serve

lemon, mint

Method

Fill a balloon glass with ice then add a 25ml mix of Freshly Foraged Elderflower Syrup and your favourite go-to Dry Gin (in a 50/50 mix).

Maybe add another 25ml shot of Dry Gin if you are feeling the need.

Next top up with the Rhunessa Rhubarb Sparkling Wine.

Fynoderee

07624 433131   www.fynoderee.com

The award-winning Fynoderee Distillery is an artisan copper-pot distillery based in the north of the Island. Founded by local couple Paul and Tiffany Kerruish, along with master distiller Gerard Macluskey, production commenced in November 2017 and the distillery has gone on to sell an astounding near 30,000 bottles in its first eighteen months of trading. Distilling initially took place at the back of Paul and Tiffany's home in Ramsey, before quickly expanding to warehouse premises in Jurby.

The name 'Fynoderee' comes from Manx folklore and is a mythical creature of the Isle of Man. He is half-man and half-goat and, as the story goes, was originally the Elfin Prince of the Island who was banished from the fairy kingdom for falling in love with a mortal girl, Kitty Kerruish. This love affair ended rather badly for all concerned and mostly took place at Glen Auldyn (just outside Ramsey), which happens to be the location where the Manx Wildlife Trust have reintroduced juniper groves to the Island. This connection to gin production, the stunning nature of the location and the coincidence of sharing a Manx surname with the main protagonist is what inspired the brand – a backstory that has been exquisitely bought to life by local artist Julia Ashby Smyth who has created all the original bottle artwork for

the distillery.

'Gin-thusiasts', Tiffany and Paul had long dreamt of setting up a distillery on the Isle of Man that would produce premium gin (and ultimately further premium spirits) using the Island's abundant wild-growing botanicals within its recipes. The couple's vision for The Fynoderee Distillery was fully formed when a chance meeting with third co-founder, Gerard Macluskey, (a former head distiller at Masons Yorkshire Gin, and before that Gordon's Tanqueray) propelled their vision into reality. Spoiled for choice in terms of local ingredients to feature in their gin, the team decided to launch with a series of seasonal gins featuring the Island's wild botanicals and showcasing Gerard's ability to create distinctive and original flavour profiles.

Each gin is an entirely different recipe – Winter is a complex and warming gin, featuring winter spices and juicy berries such as Manx sloes, elderberries and blackberries. Spring is a light and zesty affair, with fresh green herbs and Manx gorse flowers. Summer features Manx-grown strawberries in what is the sweetest of the four expressions and Autumn is the driest, with Manx apples, crab apples, wild plum, rowanberry and heather all coming together to create an earthy, dry and intensely flavoursome autumnal gin.

In addition to the seasonal range the distillery also produces a distinctive gin using chai masala spices from the Kerala region in southern India. The Kerala Chai Edition came about through a collaboration with local chef and Indian spice importer Kumar Menon, of Leela's Kitchen. This Great Taste Award-winning gin offers perfectly balanced soft chai masala spiciness on the nose, a rich and complex palate and a moreish, warming sweetness to the finish and sips particularly well with the robust flavours found in Indian and Asian cooking.

The distillery's characterful vodka, Fynoderee Manx Bumbee Vodka, gets its name from the old Manx tradition of weaving bumbee cages and the folklore surrounding them. Bumbee Vodka is produced from redistilling high-quality grain spirit with the tiniest touch of pure Manx honey. Velvety soft on the palate with a smooth, creamy finish, this is a premium vodka that can be sipped neat or mixed to bring an exciting buzz to your cocktails.

All Fynoderee spirits are created in flame-fired copper pot stills in a one-shot distillation and are hand-bottled and labelled before being distributed all over the Island, and increasingly now beyond. You will find Fynoderee products in all the best Island bars and restaurants and bottles can be ordered for Isle of Man or UK delivery from the distillery's website.

Local reaction and feedback has been incredible and the distillery is now based in a large warehouse to cope with its rapidly expanding production demand. A future move to a long-term home later this year is on the cards, where the ambitious team plan to expand its range of spirits and cater to its increasing demand for distillery tours. The team have already started whisky trials and the first barrel of Fynoderee Manx Single Malt was laid down in December 2018.

While tours are currently not possible due to size constraints, the distillery occasionally offers open evenings and is licensed for 'distillery door' sales.

Seven Kingdom Distillery

Banks Circus, Douglas, IM1 1JE
01624 620232 www.sevenkingdomdistillery.com

Seven Kingdom Distillery is a modern, forward-thinking distillery based in the heart of the capital of the Isle of Man, Douglas. The distillery is situated at the top of the North Quay in a converted industrial unit, with a restaurant and bar on site. The distillery operations all take place within the building, including distilling, bottling and labelling.

The still, which is at the heart of all operations, is named Helga, and is a 150l copper pot and column still from the Kothe factory in Eislingen, Germany. Helga is an extremely efficient still and is capable of carrying out five runs per day, meaning that at full operating capacity she can produce enough gin to fill 1200 bottles! The inclusion of the botanical basket and the catalyser means that the delicacy and nuance of flavour we can achieve is extraordinary. It also allows us to adapt the operating set-up for different styles of spirit, meaning that we can produce nearly anything with the one unit. The still, as is the case for most of the equipment, came second hand. She used to produce fruit brandies in Germany!

Seven Kingdom launched our flagship product, Douglas Dry Gin, in November 2017. The recipe comprises a mixture of international spices and

herbs, as well as hand-foraged gorse flowers, Manx heather honey, and bay. The citrus component is very forward, this is achieved through using only the freshest limes, oranges, and grapefruits. The gin's characteristic understated style screams elegance and poise, and the lingering citrus is balanced with dry spice and herbaceous notes. Douglas Dry Gin has won gold medals at competition and has become the go-to martini gin for those in the know.

Following on from the gin, Seven Kingdom Distillery launched Cronk Y Voddy Vodka – The Spirit of the Races – to coincide with TT 2018: an ultra-smooth, elegant vodka, which encapsulates the TT essence in a bottle. Alongside the ABV of 37 ¾% (the exact length of the mountain course), the vodka appeals not only to vodka aficionados, but to race enthusiasts alike. Cronk Y Voddy is named after one of the fastest stretches of the TT circuit, and is designed to be drunk straight. Easily one of the most recognisable vodka brands on the Island, the Viking logo has four horns which represent the Manx Loaghtan sheep. The wash from which the vodka was distilled was produced on Island, at the Hooded Ram Brewery, we are firm believers in doing as much as possible from scratch.

Our foray into the liqueur market came in early 2019 with the launch of Cooil Somer Rhubarb gin liqueur. The product is named for the two properties that produce the rhubarb, and is a pun on the less-than-tropical summers the Island enjoys. Both drier and stronger than most

Our emphasis has always been to produce spirits that hold their own amongst the best in the world. With the suite of products we have produced to date, our style is becoming clear – smooth, delicate, and complex. A house style of which we can be very proud.

liqueurs, Cooil Somer is perfect when added to dry sparkling wines, and is equally refreshing with tonic. Cooil Somer is also delicious drizzled over vanilla ice cream.

We provide both tours and tastings at the distillery, and these are available by request. Please email emma@sevenkingdomdistillery.com for more details.

Bath & Bottle

6 Victoria Street, Douglas, IM1 2LH
01624 845400   www.bathandbottle.com

*B*ath & Bottle is an original and boutique cocktail bar where friends can meet and drink indulgent cocktails. The atmosphere at this glamorous throwback to Prohibition-era drinking is pure nostalgia. Staff are immaculately attired, knowledgeable and passionate about their subject, and a range of vintage and rare spirits indulges those with curiosity for new drinks. We create expertly built classic cocktails along with our very own house creations.

We only use fresh ingredients in our drinks to ensure the highest quality.

Fynderella
serves 1

Ingredients

1 Staarvey Farm egg
40ml Fynoderee Manx Gin
25ml Staarvey Farm Elderflower Cordial

25ml lemon Juice
50ml Manx cucumber juice
ice cubes

Method

As with food, always source the best ingredients you can for your cocktails – preferably from your local area. It is best to use the cucumber juice as fresh as possible, so press the cucumber no more than a couple of hours before you intend to make the drink.

Start by separating the egg white from the yolk. Place the egg white in your cocktail shaker and reserve the yolk for another use

(who doesn't love creme brûlée?).

Measure the remaining ingredients into the shaker and add 1 large ice cube. Shake these ingredients together vigorously until you can no longer hear the ice cube. The mixture will now be very frothy. Add more ice to the shaker and shake again until well chilled. Taste the drink, checking for balance.

Double strain into a chilled coupette

The Island's Pantry

Train Smokers

Mobile: 243795 /416250
Facebook: Train Smokers

Our aim was to set ourselves apart from other food vendors on the Island. This we did by offering the Island something completely different and unique with our BBQ Train. It is available to hire, for corporate events and birthday parties, weddings, markets or just a good old social.

The only one of its kind in the Isle of Man, the train, looking like a mini steam train, is fuelled solely on charcoal and wood. The train on its own is an eye catcher, and becomes the focus and conversation starter at events, not to mention the tasty treats we serve from it. Alongside the train we can also do an Asado of whole lamb or pig.

All our products, where possible, are locally sourced and absolutely outstanding. The lamb from Ballakelly Farm just sets the bar for it all, as do our other meats sourced from our local butcher, Radcliffes.

Brisket and the boneless rib ciabattas are amongst the favourites, but it doesn't stop there.

We also do hefty 6oz steak burgers, pulled pork cooked low and slow and belly pork. The hot-dogs are no ordinary 'wieners' but two fat butcher's 'porkers'. For those not so keen on the meat but still want to eat the tub of Mac 'n Cheese can't be beat.

The Dairy Shed

Cooil Shee, Leodest Road, Andreas, IM7 4HA
07624 463853
thedairyshed.com

At The Dairy Shed we have been producing delicious natural yoghurt since 2016. Our yoghurt is handmade on the family-run farm based in Andreas in the Isle of Man. Fresh milk produced by our herd of Ayrshire cows

The Dairy Shed

Train Smokers

The Dairy Shed

is used to make the yoghurt, as well as supplying the Isle of Man Creamery.

Our cows graze the lush green grass of the Northern Plains of the Isle of Man from March to November and this natural and stress-free lifestyle helps our girls, all known by name and family history, to produce great quality milk. The herd is currently around 80 cows, small by some standards, but the right size we feel in order to avoid relying heavily on bought-in feed.

The Ayrshire breed, whilst not as high-yielding as other breeds, is particularly renowned for its high protein and butterfat content, making it ideal for yoghurt and cheesemaking. Milk is pasteurised and then fermented with yoghurt cultures to produce the unique fresh, lactic taste. The final stage is to strain the yoghurt, Greek-style, to give it that extra spoonability !

All of our added flavours are also freshly handmade, and it is really important to us that we use as much home-grown produce as possible. We use Manx honey, locally grown strawberries, rhubarb, blackberries and apples. With no additives and minimal sugar in our flavoured varieties, it is a healthy choice as well as a natural one.

We are proud to have won a number of Great Taste Awards for our yoghurts, the full range of which can be found in many outlets across the Isle of Man.

Our yoghurt is fully traceable with all stages from production to packaging taking place on the farm and the only food miles incurred are at the delivery stage.

Looking to the future, we are always exploring ways to grow our small family-run business in a sustainable manner, and with this in mind we are developing some exciting new products to further expand our range.

Staarvey Farm

– Salads, Herbs, Preserves
Staarvey Farm, Peel IM5 2AJ
07624 463822

Stephen's grandfather, Harold Poupart, was a market gardener and herb farmer in Surrey who sold his produce in Covent Garden. He was also the first person to commercially grow courgettes in this country and Elizabeth David had to insert an addendum into her book to take account of this fact. Stephen has fond memories of helping his grandfather on the farm, including walking into a polytunnel full of basil and smelling the fantastic fragrance.

This obviously sparked an interest in Stephen as he worked in several nurseries and garden centres, trained in Landscape and Amenity Horticulture at Writtle College, Essex, then worked his way up to become Garden Centre Manager of one of the largest Homebase Garden Centres in the UK.

Over the years we enjoyed several holidays in the Island, and Stephen had been coming here all his life, as his father is Manx, so in 2000 we decided to move over to Staarvey Farm, a three-acre smallholding near Peel, where we started growing our own herbs, fruit and vegetables using a small (60ft) polytunnel.

We enjoy natural, wholesome, quality food and wanted to share this with others on the Island.

Staarvey Farm

Stephen had always wanted his own business and so in 2006 we started selling our herbs, vegetable plants and preserves at local farmers' markets.

This enterprise has expanded over time to include six large (90–130ft) polytunnels and more land and we now grow an extensive selection of products including mixed salad leaves, micro salad, pea shoots, freshly cut herbs, edible flowers and vegetables. All our produce is organically certified by Organic Farmers and Growers and mostly grown in the ground, though we use some coir-based, Soil Association-approved, peat-free compost.

We supply many of the Island's restaurants and cafés direct, or through Robinson's, and you will also find a comprehensive range in the local Shoprite supermarkets across the Island. Additionally we supply our produce to caterers for weddings and other events.

We also produce a diverse selection of jams, marmalades, curds, chutneys, cordials, sauces and dressings, using local ingredients where possible, which are stocked in outlets across the Island – Close Leece Farm Shop, St John's; Magher Grianagh Farm Shop, Sulby; Mostly Manx, Douglas; Ronaldsway Airport, Castletown and the Welcome Centre, Sea Terminal, Douglas.

We hope you will enjoy our produce in the Island eateries, or used in your own recipes in the comfort of your home.

Paula's Kitchen

Unit 25E South Quay Douglas
07624 405320

Started from their home cottage kitchen in the beautiful village of Laxey in early 2017, Paula Garland, ably assisted by husband John, have taken Paula's passion and natural talent for creating great food to a new level. Now with two 'UK Great Taste Awards' secured (in 2018 for the Luxury Spiced Turmeric Granola and in 2019 for the Raw Trail Mix Flapjack), Paula's Kitchen products have become a staple in many households across the Island conscious of healthier eating or simply enjoying great tasting top-quality food.

When asked how it all began, Paula was quick to credit ISLEXPO 2016 (the Island's largest ever business and networking event) for providing the confidence and inspiration to set up the business. Attending the business festival and meeting other like-minded people in the food and drink industry gave Paula the motivation to transform a lifelong interest into something much more meaningful: a real family run business using ingredients of the highest quality to ensure the best possible taste and experience.

Fast forward to 2018, having moved into a new fully kitted unit at South Quay, Douglas and as the Island's only gluten-free kitchen, Paula's ethos that every ingredient she uses should be high quality and, whenever possible, sourced locally, remains key. With five unique options within the range of granolas, four types of energy balls added to the brownie, flapjack and shortbread selection as part of the 'raw food' range there

Paula's Kitchen

Paula is also quick to mention how fortunate she is to have several very supportive corporate clients who not only offer a steady business flow but provide a vital line of direct feedback and suggestions.

Paula's Kitchens next big step is to export off-Island. Having had some success in this area already the work has begun to find the best partners and local transport companies to try and take Paula's Kitchen to the next level.

Leela's Kitchen

07624 240200
www.leelaskitchen.co.uk

Kumar Menon, founder of Leela's Kitchen, has a deep family history with authentic spices. His grandfather founded Balakrishna Menon & Sons in the 1950s to trade spices through the Indian Pepper and Spice Trading Association. Instead of joining the family business in Kerala, India, Kumar wanted adventure and found that the Isle of Man not only suited his preference to cooler climates but also his love of motorbikes.

He moved to the Island in 2003 to undertake a catering course at the Isle of Man College. While sharing his family cooking with friends, he found that supermarket spices just weren't up to

really is something for everyone at Paula's Kitchen. By ensuring all products are 100% gluten-free, dairy-free, refined-sugar and additive free, they really are able to reach as many people as possible to try and buy the products. With some exciting ideas to expand the product range, and with new team members due to start soon, Paula's Kitchen has big plans for the future.

Currently, Paula's Kitchen products can be found at numerous locations across the Island and with larger businesses such as Robinson's, Riley's, Tynwald Mills and many of the EVF stores stocking the range, customers should never have too far to go to purchase their favourite items. As well as the support from the 'big stores' on Island, Paula also credits a lot of her success to the support of other small business owners. The Good Health Store in Port Erin was one of the very first businesses to stock Paula's Kitchen products and with others such as Close Leece Farm, Mother Nature and Mostly Manx also providing great support the business is now truly Island-wide.

Leela's Kitchen

Isle of Man Quinoa

Isle of Man Quinoa

01624 301863

Isle of Man Quinoa (pronounced Keen-Wah) is the Isle of Man's SUPER FOOD. For two years, James Callow and Chris Kneale have been growing the quinoa on James's farm in Cranstal, where conditions are ideal. Cranstal is blessed with lots of hot, sunny, dry days and the quinoa really thrives. James is a beef and sheep farmer, and grows some cereals for his stock, so he's well equipped to grow the quinoa, and the soil is fertile due to having livestock in the rotation. The crop is grown without any chemicals, and through the summer months the growing quinoa is alive with wildlife. Last year, when the quinoa was harvested, the ground was covered in clover that had established naturally, helping to provide the quinoa with the nutrients needed to grow.

The quinoa is harvested with a regular combine, and then dried and stored until it is needed. It then undergoes a further cleaning process before being packaged, labelled and distributed onto the shelves of local outlets across the Island.

The crop is grown in sight of the Point of Ayre lighthouse and (nearly) within a stone's throw of the sea. Some chefs have commented that they can taste the sea air in the quinoa, and we believe that this healthy environment all contributes to the taste and nutrition of the final quinoa product.

Quinoa is classed as a 'SUPER FOOD' due to its nutritional content. High in fibre, high in protein, high in amino acids, high in key minerals and antioxidants it has a numerous health benefits. It's really easy to cook and can be ready to serve in just 15–20 minutes, just add two-parts water to one-part quinoa and boil! When cooked, the quinoa has a tail that emerges, so you know when it's ready.

The cooked quinoa has a delicate and nutty flavour, and can be utilised in a wide variety of dishes from porridge and salads to cakes or used as a garnish.

scratch. Encouraged by his partner, Michele, Kumar stepped back into the world of spices, launching Leela's Kitchen in 2011, a loving tribute to his late grandmother.

Leela's Kitchen offers authentic cooking classes and a range of high quality, organic spices from turmeric to curry blends like garam masala. Leela's Kitchen spices are grown naturally, free from fertiliser, and are unique due their natural drying process. Rather than use ionised radiation to kill bacteria and prolong shelf life, Leela's Kitchen uses a process called dry frying to release natural oils, give them a more vibrant flavour and preserve the medicinal properties often destroyed in commercial irradiation.

Now partnered with the UNESCO Biosphere Isle of Man, Leela's Kitchen spices have a two-year shelf life, stored in biodegradable tubs with a completely traceable production cycle. With six Great Taste Awards and a Quality Food Award, Leela's Kitchen is a thriving award-winning Isle of Man business.

With new outlets coming on board all the time, we are really glad of the support we have received so far. You can find us on Facebook – Isle of Man Quinoa.

High Tilt Goat Dairy

High Tilt Farm, Kirk Michael IM6 1AS
07624 207555

High Tilt Goat Dairy is part of Isle of Man Goats, a farming business specialising in all things goat, set up by Clare Lewis and Mike Walker in 2012. The dairy specialises in a range of goat dairy products all made using the milk from the small herd of much-loved Anglo-Nubian goats that live on High Tilt Farm in the heart of Kirk Michael.

Anglo-Nubian goats produce the richest and creamiest milk of any goat breed. Their milk is very high in butterfat and protein, both necessary for making great cheese. You won't find this breed of goat in commercial dairies, but they are highly prized by artisan cheese makers.

The goats are milked twice a day and most of the milk is then made into cheese in the Farm's dairy. There are soft spreadable cheeses, from extremely mild, almost moussey, through to ultra-smooth with a slight goaty tang. There are various feta-style cheeses, all sold fresh, not brined, some creamy and some crumbly. Pressed cheeses are cubed and packaged in glass jars with flavoured oils, such as chilli and garlic, and a variety of herbs. Goat milk halloumi-style frying cheese includes mint leaves from the farm's kitchen garden.

Liquid goats milk is for sale and the product range is set to expand as the dairy herd numbers increase to include cream and butter, thick and creamy goat yogurt, Kefir, white mould cheeses (brie etc), and matured goats cheeses. There are even plans afoot for goats milk ice cream, which will have to be named after Gwen and Gerri who were born on the farm in 2019.

Isle of Man Goats entered the Great Taste Awards in 2019, where all four products were awarded stars and the High Tilt Cheese No4, a crumbly feta-style cheese, was given two stars. A great result for a little artisan dairy that only started making cheese in July 2018.

An increasing number of Island restaurants are using High Tilt Goat's Cheeses in their menus, showcasing the superb quality and unrivalled provenance of these truly artisan farm-produced cheeses.

Mike and Clare are passionate about the welfare of their goats and deeply committed to providing top-quality food. As well as the dairy goats, High Tilt Farm is home to South African Boer goats and angora goats. Boer goats are the world's premier meat breed, with males often growing to over 130kg in weight. The farm sells a wide range of goat meat, from a pack of chops up to a full carcass. All butchery and packing is

High Tilt Goat Dairy

carried out at the farm in the on-site butchery. Best sellers are packs of diced goat meat, perfect for an easy and authentic goat curry, minced goat, and a range of homemade goat burgers.

The angora goats produce fine mohair, which is akin to cashmere. These are sheared twice a year, and all the fleeces are graded and hand-picked on the farm before being sent to the UK to be spun. Fine laceweight knitting yarns are returned to the farm for skeining and dying, before being sold as knitting yarn or as stunning hand-knitted items, while smoother adult goat fleeces are spun into sock yarns and knitted into Manx Mohair socks.

All the products produced at High Tilt Farm are available from the Ramsey farmers' market every Saturday at the Old Courthouse in Ramsey. A farm shop is under construction and will soon provide customers with the opportunity to pop in and buy the dairy and meat straight from the farm.

High Tilt Farm opens up to the public for various events throughout the year. Keep an eye on our Facebook Pages: Isle of Man Goats, and Goga-Goat Yoga, to find out what's new at High Tilt Goat Farm.

Ballakelly Farm

Ballakelly Farm

Kiondroghad Road, Isle, of Man, IM7 3EJ
07624 492899
www.ballakelly.farm

Alan and Rachel are the real people behind Ballakelly Family Farm, located in sunny Andreas in the north of the Isle of Man. Ballakelly Farm has been farmed by our family (the Teares) for five generations.

We farm over 500 acres of grass and arable land and finish almost 3,000 top quality livestock each year. Over three years ago we decided we wanted to sell our own produce directly to the public: we wanted to receive the true rewards for the food we created on our farm. We now sell the raw products from both our farm shop at home and via the online shop with delivery service right to your door. We also sell our food 'hot' via the catering trailer and by doing hog roasts or BBQ

parties. Please visit the website and Facebook to see a full list of the things we offer.

This journey has taught us that there is a change in the mindset of people: they are starting to care more about where their food comes from, and they want to trust that what they perceive they are eating is what they are actually eating.

Our dream is to supply your family with the same quality food that we are privileged to eat around our dinner table. From farm to fork, we believe you should know exactly what you are putting in your mouth.

We have taken control of all the process from rearing the animals to transforming them into the products that you purchase from us. This means if you eat a Ballakelly product purchased directly from Farmer Al and his team, you can trust that what you are eating is 100% the best, true Manx product we could supply. Our livestock is reared on our farm and wherever possible we grow/source our suppliers on-Island to support our community and ensure traceability.

Our customers like the fact that they know the real people behind the products. Accessibility between the producer and consumer has help us build a business which has trust. We regularly have open days where we invite the general public to come and see the farm and meet the animals. Education about where your food comes from is key to our business success.

The team at Ballakelly are very passionate that we are the 'real' producers behind the products we sell. There are a lot of family and friends that have helped along the journey, they are awarded the title of 'Meat Heroes'; without these guys Ballakelly Farm would not be where it is today.

Over the last three years we have achieved 21 Taste Awards, these awards give the team at Ballakelly the confidence that we know not only are we producing a top quality product, it tastes good! We also received 'Highest Quality Assured 2018' Taste Isle of Man award, which we are really proud of, as this relates to the catering services we provide.

BallaKarran

BallaKarran

www.ballakarran.com

Will and Janette Qualtrough launched the BallaKarran brand in 2013, but its roots go much deeper. Will left school with a passion to farm instilled in him by his late uncle, Stanley Karran, and started out with a small flock of sheep on his uncle's fields at Cregneash. From the outset, Will aimed to produce and sell his own pasture-reared lamb: a sustainable, ethical product that would be completely traceable 'from farm to fork'. He chose BallaKarran as the name for his business in tribute to his Uncle Stanley.

Hard work and determination kept Will's dream on course and now BallaKarran has grown into a strong, successful company, supplying their own pasture-reared lamb along with Manx beef and pork, as well as an array of other producers'

products, to customers across the Isle of Man and further afield.

We're a true family-run business whose guiding beliefs have been consistent since the very beginning: we're passionate about the Manx countryside and contributing to our community through sustainable practice.

We're committed to high welfare standards in farming, too. All our lambs are, as nature intended, raised outdoors and reared on clover, grass and ewe's milk. There is a direct link between the quality of this upbringing and the quality of the product our customers enjoy.

During the first three years of retailing our own lamb, engaging with customers, we realised there was a demand for a variety of local Manx produce, although accessibility appeared to be a restriction. In June 2016 we discussed and researched the option of opening a shop stocking only seasonal

Davison's Ice Cream

Island produced foods. However, the ideal location did not manifest itself. We researched the idea of a mobile retail unit, as seen in certain areas of the UK and Europe, which were proving popular. The idea being to take, where possible, produce to the consumer to increase convenience. In 2017 we converted a commercial van into a bespoke butchery and farm shop.

The van, which sells 100% Manx produce, allows the team to be in the right place at the right time, serving customers in Laxey, Port St Mary, St John's, Peel, Glen Vine, Colby, Santon and the Isle of Man Business Park.

We now farm 100 ewes and a small herd of Aberdeen Angus cattle.

Believing in 100% Manx produce, and championing this, is our passion. The consumer knows where their food is coming from, it's good for the economy and it helps to ensure that we in the Isle of Man will have food security in the future.

Davison's

The Factory, Mill Road, Peel
Shops: 3 Castle Court, The Promenade, Peel
and The Chocolate Box, Castle Street, Douglas
01624 844111

Davison's has been a small family-run business since its humble beginnings making chocolates 30 years ago in the back of a small shop in the heart of Peel, on the Isle of Man. Davison's today are renowned across the Island for the range of multi-award-winning handmade Luxury Ice Cream and chocolates they produce within their state-of-the-art factory in Peel. All of the ice cream they sell is produced right here on the Isle of Man using only 100% Isle of Man double cream and butter, sourced from local dairies across the Island for their full-dairy ice cream range, and top quality dairy-alternative milks for the ever-growing non-dairy range. All of the flavourings used within the production of their ice creams are of the highest quality available and are all sourced via UK wholesalers from across Italy and France.

Today, Davison's is run by father and son, Ian and Greig, with Ian being the original founder of the company. Their main aims for the company are still the same as they were when Ian started producing ice cream 25 years ago, with the main emphasis being on producing a very high-quality product that's still affordable to everyone. Greig, after graduating from Chester University in 2010, is now head of production and produces from start to finish every drop of ice cream that leaves the premises. This hands-on involvement means that Greig is able to measure the quality of the product throughout the whole production process, allowing only the best quality products to leave the factory on a daily basis.

With ice cream being the main focus of the business now, the chocolates have taken more of a back step in the company than they would have 20 years ago. However, Davison's are still dedicated to making quality chocolate products and their small team of two are still producing these by hand within their factory premises in Peel. All of the chocolates are still produced, as they were 30 years ago, using the exact same chocolate produced by world-leading chocolate producers Barry Callebaut.

As a company, Davison's plans for the future are to explore the options available to them for entering the UK market with their products. They also have plans in the pipeline of future expansions here on the Island, however at this present time these are still under wraps and only known by a select few.

Apple Orphanage Co Ltd

The Lynague, German, IM5 2AQ
07624 439445 / 07624 315679
www.appleorphanage.com

Apple Orphanage Co Ltd is the fruit of Will Fauld's and Charlotte Traynor's labours. We press surplus local fruit from overlooked resources growing here on the Isle of Man. Sustainability and the creation of natural, innovative drinks is our aim. In 2009 we established our Fruit Exchange – the idea is pretty simple: we press your homegrown crops and in return give you a fair share of the drinks that we make from them … and for free!

We're passionate about keeping things natural and free from chemicals, so no concentrates, artificial flavourings or preservatives are used – just real, natural ingredients and fresh fruit harvested only a few miles away. We produce a range of both soft and alcoholic drinks using Manx-grown apples, rhubarb, gooseberries and other fruits/vegetables adopted through our Fruit Exchange. Our Manx apple juice is pure, unadulterated, pressed apples harvested via the Fruit Exchange. We press select apple cultivars to make a vast range of single variety juices from sweet to tangy, and nutty to floral. There's a rainbow of flavours to enjoy that showcase the hundreds of heritage apple varieties we have growing on the Isle of Man.

Our WILD Dry Cider (5.4% ABV) is also made from 100% Manx apple juice … and nothing else! Fermented using wild yeasts and slowly matured

Roots Honey

Faragher's Manx Free Range Eggs

Shore Hotel Brew Pub

And speaking of elderflower: our Elderflower Keshal (3.5% ABV) is one of our favourite summer drinks. Based on an old family recipe that we've refined over the years, it's made with fresh, Manx elderflowers harvested from right outside our barn. Our 'Keshal' (Manx Gaelic for fizz) is a wonderfully fragrant, medium dry, naturally sparkling wine with a clean citrus finish.

Shore Hotel Brew Pub

Old Laxey Hill, IM4 7DA
01624 861509

The Shore Hotel is the only public house in Old Laxey; it adjoins the River Laxey, having a 150 metre beer garden with river frontage and is just two minutes from the harbour and beach. We opened for business in April 1990 after completely renovating the bar area and changing the old Stable Bar into the Chartroom Restaurant.

In 1996 a group of local residents formed the Old Laxey Brewing Company and the Chartroom Restaurant closed for good. We commissioned Non Ferrous Fabrications Ltd from Ringwood in Hampshire to design and install a 5 brl micro-brewing plant and production commenced in February 1997.

We are the smallest independent brewery on the Island and we only brew one cask conditioned beer, Bosun Bitter ABV 3.8%. The pub bar has a nautical theme and hence our beer was christened as 'Bosun Bitter'. The Old Laxey brewery is the only brewery on the Island with its own dedicated Tap Bar which has a full public licence.

Brewery tours can be arranged by contacting Paul Phillips on 07624 336362 (mobile) or 01624 861509 (pub).

over 18–24 months, the result is a dry, light-bodied and vinous cider with a crisp apple finish and warming tannins from wild, local crab apples. Beautifully aromatic with a rich, deep apple bouquet, it is our champion!

Our range of drinks is limited only by our imagination and what we find growing on our magical Island! Our ever-growing range of sparkling, natural, soft drinks best showcase our creativity – from our classic Rhubarb Riot and Gooseberry Twist (our version of a Manx lemonade) to the vintage-inspired Gorse Cream Soda and the awesome Cherry Berry Boom (with Manx elderberries and a touch of cinnamon). We love to have fun with our drinks so you can enjoy exciting, local and delicious refreshments (and with much less sugar that mainstream soft drinks). Other seasonal, local produce we use includes pear, grape, currants, nettles, bramble leaf, mint, rosemary and elderflower.

Other Producers

Faragher's Manx Free Range Eggs - 07624 458959
Ellersile Rapeseed Oil - 07624 472717
Bushy's - 01624 661244
Roots Honey - 07624 200015
Magher Grianagh, Farm Shop, St Judes (A17) - 0762449194